INTERESTING STORIES FOR CURIOUS PEOPLE

Volume 2

*A Collection of Captivating Stories
About History, Science, Pop Culture
and Anything in Between*

BILL O'NEILL

DON'T FORGET YOUR FREE BOOKS

Contents

Introduction

Welcome to *Interesting Stories for Curious People: A Fascinating Collection of Stories Relating to History, Pop Culture, Science, and Just About Anything Else You Can Think Of*, Part Two. In this book, you'll learn about some of the strangest and most fascinating facts that make our planet a truly interesting place. Sometimes you'll laugh and at other times you'll be horrified, but you'll always be interested to see what comes next.

Among the many interesting stories you'll read are a slew of historical facts. But don't worry, if history was never your thing in school, you'll find these stories exciting and unique. Did Butch Cassidy and the Sundance Kid die in South America? Was Jesse James assassinated in his own home? How did the Romans defeat an army of elephants? These are just some of the historical topics and questions you'll read about.

You'll also learn some science facts that may seem strange but are 100% true, including the story behind the face on Mars and the facts behind some bizarre psychological conditions, such as one where people hear colors and smell sounds. You'll read about the closest planet to Earth and what may hold the best chance for life, along with a host of other facts, including the truth behind peanut allergies.

Find out about some of the strangest supernatural occurrences known to humans. These stories include what many people believe is the most haunted house in America, a couple of unearthly locations in Latin America, and more than a few creatures that witnesses claim exist.

We also dive into some quirky tales from sports and pop culture. You'll read about the life of a famous television robot, the "Ironman" of American football, the fact that there is alpine skiing in Australia, and the origins of the fakest of all sports—but I better watch out to whom I say that!

There are plenty of stories for all you true crime fans, but these aren't your average true crime stories. You'll learn about a couple of killers who were never caught, and one who still may be stalking America! A brazen heist is also profiled, along with a man who was perhaps the worst serial killer in history … and he is still on the loose!

Finally, several stories in this volume defy definition other than them just being weird. Some crossover the categories of true crime, paranormal, history, and pop culture, but their peculiar nature is why they are included in this book. These stories have no explanation, so I'll just let you decide how weird they are for yourself.

Prepare to be shocked, perplexed, and even upset, but above all, prepare to be entertained and educated at the same time!

He Comes from the
Planet Zambodia

Elvis may be the king in Memphis, Tennessee, but there is a Memphian who holds the unofficial title of the King of Weird. He goes by the name Prince Mongo and just about anyone who's had the pleasure of meeting him will tell you that he is by far the strangest man they've ever met.

Prince Mongo was born Robert Hodges and is now in his 60s, but he claims to be a 333-year-old ambassador from the planet of Zambodia. Yes, you heard that right; Prince Mongo—the name he began going by in the 1970s—claims to be from another planet. No one knows for sure if Hodges believes the crazy things he says and does, but after this many years, it's probably fair to say that, if he didn't before, he probably does by now.

And if you ever see or hear the man talk, you may be inclined to think he is from another world. Always wearing a blonde wig, aviator goggles, and flamboyant clothing, Prince Mongo has made himself as recognizable for his unique style as he has for his antics … and he has committed plenty of crazy acts since the 1970s.

It all began when Hodges wanted to bulldoze the front yard of his Memphis residence to make room for a large boat. Hodges lived in a nice, quiet Memphis neighborhood, so his neighbors resisted his unorthodox construction methods and won. The city ruled that Hodges couldn't make the changes to his yard. Hodges responded to what he perceived as an injustice by becoming Prince Mongo.

He immediately began piling dirt, old toilets, and mannequins in his front yard, calling it art and challenging the city and/or his neighbors to take him to court. Prince Mongo has lived at more than one address in Memphis, always in a nice neighborhood, and always adorns his yards with his unique style of art. The decorations have landed Prince Mongo in court more than once, but he persists and the city and his neighbors, for the most part, have given up on trying to make him comply with codes.

Many Memphians now look at him and his residences as part of the city's long and illustrious landscape. As with the Civil War to the civil rights movement, and from Elvis Presley to Prince Mongo, people in the city have come to accept Hodges for his role in the city's history.

And Prince Mongo has certainly made many conscious efforts to leave his mark on the city in several ways. Not long after his first feud with his neighbors and the city of Memphis, Prince Mongo embarked on his enduring political career and quickly shot to stardom.

He became a perennial candidate for Memphis mayor, which gained him some national media attention. He was featured in a 1980 episode of the early reality show *Real People* and more recently was in an episode of *American Pickers*. He always gives interviews in character and is always entertaining with his antics.

And the interviews are where Hodges becomes Prince Mongo. During his countless political campaigns, Mongo has never disappointed the public in living up to his persona, constantly making bizarre and controversial statements. He advocated putting sharks in the Mississippi River to stop escaping convicts and stated that public hangings should be reintroduced to downtown Memphis.

But every time Prince Mongo makes the news, people always ask: who is the real Robert Hodges? Interestingly, little is known about Prince Mongo's past. It is known that he is somehow independently wealthy—in addition to his primary Memphis residence, he owns homes in Florida and Virginia. He has also owned bars and nightclubs in Memphis. Most believe that Prince Mongo comes from family money. His brother was once the mayor of the Memphis suburb of Germantown, Tennessee.

Other Memphians think that Prince Mongo acts crazy to keep collecting on an insurance settlement. And there is a very small percentage who believe that Prince Mongo is from another planet. If you ever have the pleasure of meeting Prince Mongo, the idea that he came from another world or dimension will no doubt enter your mind!

But Did It Work?

There is a general perception that contraception is a fairly modern thing. After all, the birth control pill didn't hit the market until the 1960s and condoms weren't around until at least the 1500s, so before that time birth control consisted of the rhythm method and a lot of luck. It may seem difficult to envision a world without birth control, but you have to remember that things have changed quite a bit over the last 50 years.

Before World War II, sex was done first and foremost for procreation—pleasure was a distant second. With that said, there is documentation of birth control as far back as the New Kingdom of ancient Egypt (1500s–1095 BCE), with a lot of it sounding a little strange and some of it sounding downright nasty. But the important question is: did it work?

Medical texts from ancient Egypt show that birth control was strictly on the woman. If a couple decided that they couldn't afford to have more children, or perhaps a woman was having a sexual relationship before or apart from her marriage (yes, those things happened in ancient times as well), then she could get a prescription from a local physician. One such prescription that was documented in a medical book states:

Beginning of the prescriptions prepared for wives to allow a woman to cease conceiving for one year, two years or three years: *qaa* part of acacia, carob, dates: grind with one *henu* (450 ml) of honey, lint is moistened with it and place in her flesh.

The flesh being described is the patient's vagina. Examples from other Egyptian texts describe similar contraception prescriptions, with some relating some more details, such as: "the lint should be placed at the mouth of the uterus." In most of these texts, honey is the active ingredient, which leads one to question if the Egyptians were on to something.

Modern experts are divided on honey's efficacy as a contraceptive ingredient. Most experts believe that if the prescriptions were successful, it was totally due to luck or other factors. However, some contend that the honey may have been spermicidal through an osmotic effect.

The reality is that most ancient Egyptian birth control prescriptions were more than a little nasty and some were very unhygienic. Although contraceptive prescriptions that used honey were the most common, many other substances were used, including crocodile dung! Yes, you read that correctly—crocodile poop was used as a contraceptive.

Based on this information, it very well may be that ancient Egyptian contraceptive prescriptions were very effective, but not due to the prescriptions doing what they were intended. No, the scent of these prescriptions was likely enough to kill any intimate mood or sexual desire altogether. There were probably a lot of women *and* men with headaches in ancient Egypt.

Go Break a Leg

Every human language is unique, full of plenty of nuances and idioms that sound strange to a non-native speaker. Even people fluent in more than one language often have a difficult time with the slang, idioms, and vernacular expressions of their second language. If you don't grow up with a particular language, then you just won't understand how to use some words and phrases because they often don't make sense.

Native speakers rarely question the idioms and slang they use, while those newer to the language may overanalyze certain expressions. One such expression in English that boggles non-native speakers, and rightfully so, is the idiom "break a leg."

As you probably know, the term is often used in the entertainment industry to wish someone luck before performing. Over the years, it has also been said to send good fortune to one embarking on a host of different ventures. So, what is the origin of this illogical idiom and why has it become so popular?

It's generally been believed that "break a leg" first became popular in the American theater during the 1930s as a way for actors to wish each other luck before going on stage. Since actors are traditionally a superstitious bunch, it was believed that simply telling a colleague "good luck" could have the opposite effect. So, to avoid tragedy on the stage, actors began consciously turning things around by telling each other to "break a leg."

Although this is all verified by evidence, the true origins of the term are probably much older and more complex. One theory holds that the idiom didn't originally come from superstition but was instead a reference to taking a bow after a good performance. Stage actors traditionally bow after a successful performance, and although today they do so by bending their torso forward, in the 1700s and 1800s the bows were much more involved—or dare I say, theatrical. Male actors would often bow with one leg noticeably forward, while female actors would curtsy. Both elaborate bows required the actors to bend, or "break," their knees.

Another potential early origin for the idiom has to do with the edge of the stage being known as the "leg." If you made it onto the stage for a scene, you were said to "break the leg." In the 1800s, this was important because it was often the only way you were paid as an actor—understudies and stand-ins were sore out of luck!

The fact that adoring audiences often flung coins onto the stage during good performances may also have played a role in the idiom's origins. In early theater, if a cast put on a particularly good performance, the audience would throw coins and other valuable items onto the stage, which the actors would collect by bending their knees.

Finally, "break a leg" has been ascribed a more notorious origin by some who argue that it was coined by President Abraham Lincoln's assassin, John Wilkes Booth. According to the legend, Booth claimed in his diary that, after shooting the president and making his escape by jumping to the stage below, he broke his leg in the process. There is also a theory that the English expression "break a leg" was influenced by the German idiom "Hals und Beinbruch" (neck and leg break) that was common among fighter pilots in World War I and II.

Most historians and people associated with the stage are adamant that the expression "break a leg" is purely a superstition that began in the 1930s, but it seems likely that it was influenced by several different sources.

I've Seen Him Before,
I Know It!

Have you ever thought that you keep seeing the same person wherever you go? The person may be dressed differently, or even have a different look, but you could swear that it is the same person, just wearing a disguise. You go to the supermarket and there is that guy you saw earlier at the bus stop. Then later, you're at your favorite coffee shop and you see him again, only this time he's working in the kitchen. Even worse, have you ever traveled thousands of miles, to another state or even another country, to see that same guy walking around the airport when you arrive?

If you've had this happen to you once or twice in your life, don't worry—this sort of thing can happen to anyone. Since most people fit a certain phenotype or "look," we tend to notice things in familiar people; therefore, we may occasionally think we're seeing the same person in different places and times, even when we're not. But if it is something that happens frequently then you may be suffering from the rare psychological disorder known as Fregoli delusion.

Fregoli delusion was first identified and named in the 1920s by psychiatrists who treated a 27-year-old British woman who believed she was being persecuted by a couple of actors. According to the afflicted woman, the actors kept changing their appearances in their relentless pursuit of her. Of course, the woman was delusional, and as the affliction was newly identified and quite novel, it was named for Italian actor Leopoldi Fregoli, who was known for his ability to change his appearance throughout a production. Fregoli delusion is no joke, though, for those suffering from it.

Those suffering from Fregoli delusion have problems with their associative nodes. We all have associative nodes in our brains and for the vast majority of us they work properly. Associative nodes help us link a familiar face or place, which reminds us of someone or something when we see someone or something new. For those afflicted with Fregoli delusion, though, there is a problem with their associative nodes, leading them to think that similar-looking people or places *are* the person or place they've seen before.

Needless to say, Fregoli delusion can be quite debilitating. Sufferers of the rare disorder often believe they are being persecuted by some vast, elaborate conspiracy, and when pressed for details, other elements of the disorder are manifested. For instance, not only do Fregoli delusion sufferers see the same people wherever they go, they often also see the same places or even events.

For someone with Fregoli delusion, everyday life can seem like a big joke is being played on them, or that there is some mysterious, nefarious puppet master pulling the strings of their lives. This can create a lot of confusion for the afflicted and those trying to help them, even for those with moderate cases of Fregoli delusion. The good news about Frigoli delusion is that, although it is very rare, it can be treated with antipsychotic drugs.

The bad news about Frigoli delusion is that the exact causes remain unknown and it remains understudied by academics and professionals. It also appears that the disorder may begin afflicting some people later in their lives, which means that it is more difficult to identify. Also, people who manifest Frigoli symptoms later in their lives tend to be less likely to seek professional help. Would you go to the doctor if you thought someone was following you around?

The Legend Behind the Hockey Team's Name

If you're an American sports fan, then you probably know a little about the National Hockey League (NHL) team, the New Jersey Devils. You may know that the New Jersey Devils call Newark, New Jersey their home and that they play in the Eastern Conference of the NHL. You may also know that in the team's relatively young life (it didn't become the current club until 1982), it has won three Stanley Cup trophies, which is the championship in that league.

So, the New Jersey Devils have an impressive sports pedigree, but have you ever thought about the team's nickname? Chances are, you probably just thought "devils" was a cute or clever name for the team's mascot. After all, only so many teams can be named the bears, tigers, or lions, right? Well, the name has a connection to a bizarre New Jersey legend known as the Jersey or Leeds Devil.

It is a legend that has grown over the decades and has become as much a part of the local lore of rural New Jersey as its American Revolutionary War past. Most people think the Jersey Devil is pure legend, while others believe that there are some—as of yet unidentified—creatures flying around the Pine Barrens of New Jersey.

According to the legend, a deformed-looking creature—or creatures—prowls the isolated New Jersey Pine Barrens at night looking for victims. It has been described as having a horse or goat head, bat wings, the body of a horse, and two hooved horse legs that it uses to walk bipedally. It is usually described as being leery of people, although it has also been accused of attacking people on more than one occasion.

Since the 1700s, New Jersians have reported seeing this creature, which they eventually began referring to as the Jersey Devil. The creature's origins, though, are just as confusing and bizarre as the descriptions of the creature itself.

According to one legend, a Pine Barren resident known as Jane Leeds was tired of having children. Leeds already had 12 children that she and her husband had a difficult time feeding, so when she learned she was pregnant with a 13th child in 1735, she cursed the child. It was truly unlucky 13. The story continues that, although the child was born seemingly normal, it eventually morphed into the Jersey Devil and began terrorizing the locals.

Another version of the Jersey Devil's origins may be related to the family of 17th-century New Jersey mystic Daniel Leeds. Leeds earned quite a reputation as a mystic and a pro-monarchy activist during a time when both were considered unpopular and even blasphemous by many in southern New Jersey. Daniel's son, Titan, was even described as a monster and a ghost by none other than Benjamin Franklin, who was a business competitor of the Leeds. It also just so happened that the Leeds family prominently displayed their family crest, which featured a dragon-like creature with bat-like wings.

Whatever the origins, sightings of the strange creature were reported throughout the 1800s, with farmers often claiming that the Devil was responsible for killing livestock. Reports of the creature stalking the Pine Barrens were sporadic until

January 1909 when a flurry of disturbing events was reported throughout New Jersey and the neighboring states of Pennsylvania, Delaware, and Maryland.

During the week of January 16 to 23, 1909, when most New Jersians were trying to keep warm in the dead of winter, the Jersey Devil wanted people to know that he was still around. Among the several sightings of that week were claims that it attacked a residence, a trolley car, and that it even left its hoof prints in the snow. Armed citizen patrols were formed to find and kill the Devil, but almost as quickly as the sightings started, they ended.

Sporadic sightings of the Jersey Devil have continued to the present, but most people are skeptical. Experts claim that the majority of sightings can be attributed to a combination of factors. Several of the claims are probably outright hoaxes.

One of the more elaborate hoaxes took place in 1909 when two men purchased a kangaroo and then attached fake wings and claws to it. They then advertised the animal as the Jersey Devil and charged admission to see it at a private museum. In case you're wondering, yes, people did pay to see the kangaroo and yes, many left believing they had just seen the Jersey Devil. Most of the other hoaxes are probably little more than people pulling pranks by calling in a sighting to the local media.

Experts believe that most of the Jersey Devil sightings are simply cases of over-active imaginations. The Pine Barrens is a pretty isolated, desolate place and when contrasted with the hustle and bustle of the rest of New Jersey, some of its sights and sounds can seem pretty strange to the average urbanite. The Pine Barrens is also home to several large mammals that the average city dweller does not usually see, including deer, bears, and bobcats. More than likely, many of the Jersey Devil sightings were one of these animals running across the road.

But, of course, not every sighting can be explained as a hoax or someone's imagination. So, if you ever have the chance to drive through the Pine Barrens at night, especially on one of its more isolated two-lane roads, listen and look carefully. That shadow you see leaping across the road may just be the Jersey Devil.

The Hollywood Ripper

Hollywood is a place where many dreams begin for countless people from all over the world. They travel to Tinseltown to make it big in film or television, and to "get seen" while they work regular jobs in bars, restaurants, and stores. Hollywood is also a place where many dreams end.

Many of the young people who come to southern California with stars in their eyes are quickly confronted with the cold reality that beneath the glamor is a very cold, cruel city. Many young hopefuls become drug-addicted, then turn to sex work and crime to feed their habit or pay the rent.

In between the hopefuls with stars in their eyes and the ones who have been utterly defeated are people like Ashley Ellerin. Ashley was a 20-year-old hopeful actor and artist who had a nice little bungalow a block from the famous Chinese Theatre. She was a fashion design student and worked part-time as a stripper to pay the fairly high rent, but she was always looking to step up in life. She thought she did that when she met A-list actor Ashton Kutcher in early 2001.

Ellerin had a date with Kutcher on February 21, 2001, but unfortunately for her, she met up with the Hollywood Ripper that night. The Ripper stabbed Ashley 47 times and left her bloody, broken body to be discovered later by her roommate. It wasn't the Hollywood Ripper's first kill and it wouldn't be his last.

Michael Gargiulo came to Hollywood from the Chicago, Illinois area in 1999 with dreams of fame and fortune. He told friends and family—and just about anyone who would listen—how he was going to be a major action star. Most people just humored Gargiulo, thinking that his fantasies would subside and he'd get back to reality. But the reality is that Gargiulo harbored some pretty dark, twisted fantasies.

Gargiulo's journey to Hollywood, and his transition to becoming the Hollywood Ripper, began in 1993 in his hometown of Chicago when he was just 17. On the night of August 13 of that year, it is believed that Gargiulo claimed his first victim when he stabbed an 18-year-old woman named Tricia Pacaccio to death on her backdoor step. The crime shocked the quiet neighborhood, and although many neighbors thought that the culprit was an outsider, the police had a good idea that it was someone who knew Tricia. She hadn't been robbed and wasn't sexually assaulted, although it appeared that there was a struggle. To the police, the crime didn't look random and it didn't look like a robbery.

Gargiulo was a friend of Tricia's brother and was familiar with the home, so he was immediately questioned by the police. After Gargiulo gave some conflicting statements to the police and acted suspiciously immediately after Tricia's murder, he became a suspect but was never arrested. When the investigation stalled, Gargiulo took the opportunity to move to southern California in 1999, telling his friends and family that he was going to pursue his lifelong dream.

Only he never told anyone that his real dream was brutally murdering as many women as possible. From 1999 until June 6, 2008, Gargiulo moved around southern California working as a heating and air conditioning installer and repairman. He had many live-in girlfriends, developed a social network and, by all accounts, appeared to be a normal guy. But underneath the surface was a rage that he could barely contain.

"I left the bitch on the steps for dead," Gargiulo once told a couple of friends in California. He was bragging to the men about having committed a murder and was referencing Tricia's murder in Chicago, but neither of the men took him seriously. Few people who knew Gargiulo took him seriously. He bragged about being in movies that he wasn't in and continually told stories that made him seem tougher or cooler than he was. So, in a city that is full of plastic, fake people, Gargiulo for the most part went unnoticed.

But Gargiulo's bragging nearly caught up with him when he became a suspect in Ashley Ellerin's murder. The Los Angeles Police even took a DNA sample. It didn't tie him directly to Ashley's murder but was a match for DNA taken from underneath Tricia Pacaccio's fingernails. It would seem like it would've been enough for the Chicago Police to arrest him, but they reasoned that, since they knew each other, it could have come from consensual contact. The situation presented Gargiulo with another opportunity to add to his Hollywood Ripper resume.

On December 1, 2005, he stabbed his neighbor, 32-year-old Maria Bruno, to death as she slept in her El Monte, California apartment. The Ripper was careful not to leave any DNA evidence behind in that crime, although one of the medical booties he was wearing was later found by the police in the parking lot of the complex.

The Hollywood Ripper then attacked another neighbor of his in Santa Monica on April 28, 2008. Michelle Murphy was similar to Gargiulo's other victims—she was young, attractive, and most importantly, she lived alone. As he did with the previous two victims, the Hollywood Ripper crept into Murphy's bedroom as she slept and began stabbing into her flesh.

But instead of quickly killing his prey, the Ripper was surprised when Murphy fought back. Gargiulo eventually gave up the fight and left, not before—strangely—apologizing. He left Murphy near death, but she ultimately survived, and because she fought back, some of Gargiulo's DNA was left on her.

The DNA was quickly matched to samples in the database and Gargiulo was arrested. After several years of pre-trial shenanigans on Gargiulo's part, a trial finally commenced where Gargiulo was convicted of first-degree murder. In October 2019, a jury recommended the death penalty but, at the time of writing, the sentence is still waiting to be granted by a judge.

Although Gargiulo will never be free to kill again, there are still a lot of unanswered questions surrounding the Hollywood Ripper. The first is, how could one police department make such a big mistake? A retired Chicago homicide detective admitted that their unwillingness or inability to do anything about the Tricia Pacaccio case allowed the Hollywood Ripper to hunt women in southern California, noting "Those young women in California are dead because we dropped the ball."

Perhaps an even bigger question is: are there more victims? By committing three murders, this officially makes Gargiulo a serial killer, but based on statements he made to the press, some believe he may have as many as ten more victims. His method of operation was certainly distinct, but southern

California is a very, very big place. Perhaps after cooling his heels in the California state prison system for a while the Hollywood Ripper may want to talk.

Robot or Robby the Robot?

Science fiction first became a popular genre of fiction during the 1950s. After the Soviets launched the first artificial satellite, they also started the Space Race with the United States, which soon became a major part of American pop culture. Science fiction themed comic books, films, and later television shows that pondered human space exploration became extremely popular with kids during the 1950s and '60s.

The plots and special effects of many of these movies and TV shows are silly and cheesy when you watch them today. They were based on a concept of space travel that was much more fantasy than reality, which can make them fun to watch today, though not necessarily in a thought-provoking way.

If you've watched enough sci-fi films and TV shows from that period, you know that one of the more humorous things is what the writers thought robots would look like in the future. Sometimes, they were vaguely anthropomorphic, they almost always moved slowly, and they always spoke like someone talking into a fan.

And, if you've watched enough of those shows, you've probably noticed that two Hollywood robots got more roles than all others—"Robot" and "Robby the Robot." The two prop robots looked very similar, were in similar shows, and sounded alike, but they had different lives!

Robby the Robot is the older of the two robots, having first appeared in the 1956 film *Forbidden Planet*. Robby, short for robot, was designed by the art department at MGM studios as a somewhat human-looking robot of the future. He was bipedal, with two arms and clamps for hands. His head was comprised of several switches, levers, and lights encased in plexiglass. An actor would get inside the suit to give it movement.

Robby's anthropomorphic look and solid performance in *Forbidden Planet* landed him several more important roles in film and television. He starred in four episodes of *The Twilight Zone* and demonstrated great acting range with bit parts in comedy sitcoms such as *Hazel*, *The Many Loves of Dobie Gillis*, and *Holmes & Yo-Yo*. But perhaps Robby's greatest role was when he faced off against his successor, Robot.

After the success of Robby the Robot, Hollywood prop artist Robert Kinoshita, who was the primary designer of Robby, built a new robot that took some of the ideas from Robby, while adding a few new twists. This new robot became simply known as "Robot" and starred in the hit American television show *Lost in Space* from 1965 to 1968. Although Robot had a similar basic look to Robby, there were notable differences. Robot had two legs, but they were covered with bellows, causing the robot to move on wheels. Like Robby, Robot also had a see-through plexiglass head, but his was smaller and looked like a gumball machine. Robot was metallic, as was Robby, but Robby was a darker color.

Robot was given plenty of personality by the writers of *Lost in Space*, which was brought out by actor Bob May, who was inside the Robot prop costume in some scenes. Robot appealed to the young demographic just as C-3PO would decades later. A stunt double of the Robot was also made for more dangerous scenes. But as much as Robot may have been physically tough, since *Lost in Space* was a kids' show he tended to use his mind over his brawn.

So, you're probably wondering, or maybe not: which robot would win in a fight? Well, that was somewhat answered in two episodes of *Lost in Space* when Robot defeated his rival. But don't feel bad for Robby the Robot. He had a long career as a bit part actor and did many cameos. He was sold to a private collector in 2017 for more than $5 million … now, that's not bad!

As for Robot, unfortunately, he didn't have quite the career as his older brother. The stunt double Robot now sits somewhere in storage at the Science Fiction Museum and Hall of Fame in Seattle, Washington, where access is limited. The Robot costume Bob May wore was bought by television producer Kevin Burns and now sits in his private collection.

Who knows, maybe the current owners will arrange a reunion for the robots. I'm sure sci-fi fans would want to see that!

This Diamond Is a Man's Best Friend

The sport of baseball is America's pastime and its number one sports export to the rest of the world. Baseball is played extensively in many Asian and Latin American countries and in recent years has grown in popularity in Australia, South Africa, and some European countries. You only have to look at a Major League roster to see that baseball has truly become an international sport.

But one of the things that people not familiar with baseball find so strange about the sport is that it seems to have a language of its own. A softly hit fly ball that falls for a hit is often called a blooper *or* a Texas Leaguer, a double play is also known as a "twin killing," and a home run can be a dinger, round-tripper, or a bomb.

Perhaps the most interesting, and important, slang in baseball is the name for the playing field—the diamond. If you're not familiar with the sport, a baseball playing field includes four bases that a player must round to score a point—or run, as it is called. The player does this by putting the ball into play by hitting it with the bat and then running from home base around the other three bases and back to home base to score the run. Each base is defended by an opposing player, and there is a pitcher who throws the ball to the batter, and an extra infielder as well. There are also three defenders in the outfield.

The part of the field with the bases is known as the infield, and if you take a look at it, it sort of resembles a diamond. A factor that makes baseball such an interesting sport to many is how the dimensions of the baseball diamonds range from field to field. Unlike other major team sports where there are strict codes concerning the size and dimensions of the playing fields, baseball diamonds usually only have to have certain general dimensions. Even in Major League Baseball, there is a fair amount of range in the size and the dimensions of stadiums.

The infield diamond is required to be a square with 90 feet on each side and there must be a minimum of 325 feet from home plate to the nearest wall. The center-field fence/wall, the farthest point from home plate to the fence/wall, must be a minimum of 400 feet. The bases, or plates, as they are known, must also be a certain size. Other than that, there is great leeway allowed in stadiums.

For instance, the size of outfield walls varies greatly and so do the foul ball areas between first and third baselines and the dugouts. These differences have led to some unique variations in some ballparks, such as the fabled Green Monster of Fenway Park in Boston, which results in home teams having a considerable advantage in baseball.

Baseball may seem like a confusing sport to the uninitiated due to its gameplay, use of slang terms, and playing field, but all of that is what makes it so popular with millions of people around the world. Being a baseball fan and player is like being part of a fraternity where a different type of diamond is a precious commodity.

A Mysterious
American Monument

If you've ever been to the Miami suburb of Homestead, Florida there's a good chance you've visited, or at least heard of, the Coral Castle. Unfortunately, since Florida is known for its many kitsch tourist traps that include numerous places called Gator Land and spots that claim to be authentic Seminole villages, the Coral Castle is often overlooked.

The Coral Castle is a collection of several large pieces of oolite limestone in the form of chairs, tables, a working sundial, an eight-foot tall perimeter wall, and a two-story "castle" where the park's enigmatic creator, Edward Leedskalnin (1887–1951), lived. Although the park has a definite character and charm, what makes it so amazing is the mystery surrounding Leedskalnin and how the park was built.

Leedskalnin was a native Latvian who immigrated to the United States in the early 1900s. Like most other immigrants of that period, Leedskalnin thought that by immigrating to America he could find fortune and happiness. Instead, he quickly found out that the streets in America weren't paved with gold. After traveling around the country for several years looking for work, Leedskalnin contracted tuberculosis, which led him to find relief in Florida. It was there that the mystery of the Coral Castle began.

Leedskalnin turned to alternative medical treatments for his tuberculosis, particularly magnetic therapy. As he treated himself using magnets, Leedskalnin also bought some land in Florida City, Florida in 1923 and began work on the Coral Castle. The introverted Latvian immigrant slowly but surely built a park that attracted people from around Florida and, eventually, the world. But what is most amazing about this story is not what Leedskalnin built, but *how* he did it.

The recluse was never known to have hired anyone to help him quarry the stones, nor to help him move the entire park to its current location in 1936. This is pretty incredible when one considers that the Coral Castle is comprised of 1,100 stones ranging in weight from eight to 27 tons, with an average of around 15 tons.

An eight-foot revolving stone block, which could be moved by a child with the touch of a finger, served as the entrance to the mysterious edifice. There are few logical, rational explanations as to how he was able to do it or even why it was built.

It is believed that Leedskalnin built the structure as a monument to a lost love in Latvia, but the methods he used remain a mystery and he was always circumspect when asked by locals or reporters. He once said that he used a "perpetual motion holder" to move the blocks but never elaborated on the specifics of that tool. A couple of teenagers claimed to have seen Leedskalnin levitating some blocks one day and others have said that he had some arcane knowledge of magnetism, but none of that can be proven.

If pressed about his building methods, Leedskalnin would only respond: "I understand the laws of weight and leverage and I know the secrets of the people who built the pyramids."

Again, he never elaborated on what those secrets are and how they relate to the knowledge of pyramids that was understood at the time he made that statement.

Some were hopeful that the secrets of the Coral Castle would be revealed when the revolving entrance door quit working in 1986. The door/block was taken out and it was discovered that a steel rod ran through a drilled hole and rested on a truck bearing. The owners had the pieces replaced, but it quit working again about 20 years later.

Today, the Coral Castle attracts curious visitors from all over the world who want to catch a glimpse of one of the modern world's greatest mysteries. Engineering experts, scientists from different disciplines, historians, and everyday people continue to argue how the Coral Castle was built, but we aren't any closer to knowing the answer today than we were in 1936.

Perhaps some mysteries were never meant to be solved.

A Familiar Flag

A modern national flag is a symbol of a country and people. It serves as both a beacon and a source of pride. Most modern flags are fairly new in terms of world history, having been created in the 1700s or later. Some of the better-known national flags are immediately recognizable to people of any nationality. For instance, the British Union Jack is well-known because of Britain's world dominance in the 1800s—and more recently, due to James Bond films—while the United States flag is currently probably the more recognized flag.

Very similar to the United States flag is the flag of Liberia. If you're reading this and wondering, "where is Liberia?", don't worry, you're not alone. Liberia is a small west-central African country that has been plagued by poverty, corruption, and civil war since its inception in 1847, but it is noticeable for its unique—yet not so unique—national flag.

You see, at first glance, Liberia's national flag almost looks like the spitting image of the U.S. flag. It has red and white stripes with a blue canton in the upper left corner and a white star. A closer look reveals, though, that it is slightly different from Old Glory. Instead of 13 stripes, it has 11, and instead of 50 stars in the canton, there is only one. Still, the Liberian national flag's similarity to the American flag is remarkable, which raises the question: why?

Well, despite being located thousands of miles away from the United States, Liberia has a very American history. When slavery was still being practiced in the U.S., there was plenty of opposition to it, but those opposed had varying reasons. You might be surprised that the abolitionists who believed Blacks were equal to Whites and should be given full political equality were the minority. Most people who opposed slavery did so because they didn't want to compete against slave labor; they were not necessarily interested in helping Black people.

These people were called the Free Soil movement, and although they were very much against slavery, they were also against racial equality. The Free Soilers primarily wanted to keep slavery from spreading into the western territories and states but didn't care about its status in the South.

Perhaps the greatest number of abolitionists believed that slavery was wrong, for moral and economic reasons, but that Blacks could never be fully integrated into American society. Some argued that Blacks were inferior, and others said that Whites would never accept them, while most thought a little of both. As influential abolitionists with these ideas got together, they came up with the idea of repatriating slaves and former slaves back to Africa. Repatriation organizations began forming in the early 1800s, with the American Colonization Society (ACS) being the most prominent.

The ACS bought land in western Africa in the 1820s, and shortly thereafter the first freed American Blacks began arriving in west Africa to build a new society. It would be a Black society on African soil, but since the former slaves only knew American culture, it would also be a society with heavy American influence.

By 1847, the colony of Liberia declared its independence, with American born Joseph Jenkins Roberts as its first president. Due to Liberia's American heritage, Jenkins and the nation's other founding fathers chose the American flag as the template for their new flag. The 11 stripes represent the 11 men who signed the Liberian Declaration of Independence, with the rest of the flag following pretty close to the American pattern.

Although the American–Liberian influence has diminished in recent decades, as the Americo–Liberian ethnic group (those descended from African-American slaves) has lost its hold of political power and is a small minority, the government of Liberia has shown no signs of changing the flag. The people of Liberia take pride in their red, white, and blue flag, which stands apart from most other African flags that have a dominant green color theme.

What Happened to the Crew of the Kaz II?

The ocean can be a pretty scary, foreboding, and unpredictable place. One minute, it can appear calm and peaceful, and then suddenly turn into a deadly force that you can't escape. There's a reason why ancient people all had sea gods and why long-distance sea travel was something only the bravest did until relatively recent times.

We like to think that we've conquered the oceans, but now and then the oceans strike back to show us who's in control. In April 2007, the ocean decided to let three Australian men know who was boss. It swallowed them into its depths but left their yacht, the *Kaz II*, to be found. But when the *Kaz II* was found, it only seemed to raise more questions than answers. It remains one of the greatest maritime mysteries in history.

It was supposed to be the trip of a lifetime for *Kaz II* owner Derek Batten (56) and his friends, brothers Peter Tunstead (69) and James Tunstead (63). Batten bought the 32-foot catamaran to sail with his two friends from Queensland near the scenic Great Barrier Reef around the northern coast of Australia back to their homes in Perth, Western Australia. The trip was expected to take about two months, but it was over almost as soon as it began.

The trio left Airlie Beach, Queensland on their voyage on April 15, 2007, and they were never seen again. The authorities found the boat adrift on April 20 just outside the Great Barrier Reef and towed it ashore, which proved to be the beginning, or the end, of the mystery.

The boat was fully stocked with food, a gun and ammunition were present, and there were no signs of a struggle—no blood was found and nothing on the boat was destroyed. Fishing lines and laundry were set out, indicating that the men didn't plan to leave and that whatever happened to them happened very quickly.

As news of the *Kaz II* was reported, it didn't take long for several theories to circulate. The sexy and salacious theories included pirates and insurance policies. One theory held that, since the *Kaz II*'s fenders were out, it indicated that it had contact with another boat and that the other boat had some bad guys who kidnapped and killed the three men. The police quickly shot down this theory, though, pointing out that some sailors leave their fenders down at all times and that there were no signs of a struggle. Also, nothing of value was taken from the boat.

Another extreme theory held that the men had faked their deaths to collect insurance benefits. All three men were financially stable, however, and there is absolutely no evidence of fraud. There have been no signs of the men in the years since, such as sightings or financial activities.

After investigating the boat and interviewing witnesses who last saw the men, as well as their friends and family, Queensland coroner Michael Barnes determined that it was a series of very unlucky incidents that led to all three men's deaths. Barnes stated in a hearing that it all began when one of the men got a fishing line tangled in the boat's rudder. One of the two brothers tried to untangle the line but fell into the water, which panicked his brother who then dove in to save him. At that point, Batten attempted to go back for his friends by dropping the sails, but the boom swung around and put him in the water with the brothers.

"Once the three men were in the water there was very little chance they could get back on the boat," Barnes said. "It would be beyond their reach in seconds. From that point, the end would have been swift."

If they didn't drown, the great white sharks would've had them for lunch. It was just the ocean's way of letting humans know who's still in charge.

Very Valuable Boobs

Cosmetic surgery has become a very big industry in industrialized countries, and if you happen to be a plastic surgeon or know one then you probably already know that. Countless women and many men have paid for plenty of plastic surgeons' second homes, sports cars, and mistresses, with their facelifts, nose jobs, and of course, breast implants.

Breast implants have been done since the 1960s, but it was the 1980s when they ballooned into what they are today. Breast implants remain popular with women who aren't happy with their natural size or shape, as well as women who had to undergo mastectomies due to breast cancer.

But the cost of getting breast implants is no joke! Women pay between US$5,000 and $10,000 for the procedure, depending upon the doctor's reputation, what country they are in, and if the implants are saline or silicone. But in 2016 the world learned of a woman who got a free pair of breast implants and was even going to be paid for them. The catch was, she had to fill the implants with cocaine and bring them from Colombia to Germany.

In March 2016, customs officials at the international airport in Frankfurt, Germany became suspicious of a young woman who had just arrived from Colombia. The fact that Colombia is a primary point of origin for many drug smugglers already made the officials pay closer attention, but when they noticed she was sweating and fidgeting, she was brought in for secondary questioning. Once in the interview room, the woman complained that she was in severe pain from a recent breast implant surgery.

The customs officials then examined the woman, quickly noticing that the implants were more likely done by a butcher than a plastic surgeon. The woman had large, noticeable scars on her chest and breasts, which led them to think that she was a drug mule carrying the stash most uniquely. The officials had seen mules come through their airport with drugs in their stomachs but never in their breasts.

The woman was brought to a local hospital where the makeshift implants were removed, and lo and behold, instead of saline or silicone implants, the Colombian woman had an approximate one-pound bag of cocaine in each breast. The street value of the dope implants was estimated to be about US$225,000. Now those were some very expensive boobs!

My Foot Fell Asleep

You've no doubt felt the sensation of having your foot, arm, or hand "fall asleep" at some point in your life. The feeling of pins being pushed into your skin is unpleasant, but fortunately, it passes pretty quickly ... most of the time. The sensation is part of a medical phenomenon known as paresthesia, which for most people is a transitory feeling of unpleasantness, but for some is a chronic condition of pain.

Paresthesia is simply a tingling in the skin that can have a variety of causes. The most common form of paresthesia happens when pressure is applied to a nerve over an extended period, such as sleeping on your arm or sitting cross-legged for too long. Taking pressure off the nerve usually makes the sensation go away within minutes. This is pretty natural and happens frequently, but there are other times when paresthesia signals something more serious.

Paresthesia is generally associated with neurological conditions, although it can also be a sign of circulatory problems. Mercury poisoning, herpes infection, and plaque ruptures can all be causes of chronic paresthesia. If you are afflicted with chronic paresthesia, no matter how much you rub your limb that has fallen asleep, it won't seem to get much better because more serious problems are taking place in the body.

For the vast majority of you reading this, though, don't worry the next time your foot falls asleep—just rub it some and wait a few minutes. It's only a pinched nerve.

Scipio Versus Hannibal

There have been many great military generals in world history, although few have faced off against each other. During the Second Punic War (218–201 BCE) between Rome and Carthage, two of the greatest generals of all time faced each other in a heavyweight battle that determined who would rule the western Mediterranean basin.

In one corner was Hannibal Barca, the no-nonsense, tough-as-nails general of the Carthaginian military. He was a true man's general, who fought alongside his troops and led from the front. Although part of the Carthaginian elite, Hannibal wasn't afraid to get dirty and hang out with the rank-and-file of his troops, which endeared him to his army.

In the other corner was Publius Cornelius Scipio. Don't let his middle name fool you—he too was a tough military leader who earned the respect of his troops. Scipio was born to a privileged Patrician Roman family but proved his worth as a young man both in the military and in the halls of the Roman Senate, which could be just as dangerous.

In normal times, the two men probably could've been good friends. But the 3rd century BCE wasn't a normal time. You see, Hannibal was driven by hatred of Rome. His father, Hamilcar, led Carthage against Rome in the First Punic War (264–241 BCE), which ended in disaster for Carthage. The Carthaginians were humiliated and lost many of their colonial possessions to the Romans, including Sicily. Many Carthaginians were fine with the situation, but Hamilcar wasn't and vowed to do whatever he could to restore Carthage's former glory.

Hamilcar led the Carthaginian's efforts to organize colonies on Spain's Mediterranean coast, which eventually put them on another collision course with Rome. Before he died, Hamilcar instilled a healthy dose of hatred of Rome in his son Hannibal and made him promise that he would make it his life's mission to destroy Rome. Hannibal readily agreed to be his father's tool of vengeance.

In 218 BCE, after a border skirmish broke out between Carthage and Rome in Spain, Hannibal led an army of more than 100,000 men and 37 elephants—yes, I said elephants!— from Spain across the Alps into Italy.

The Romans sent army after army to stop Hannibal, but they always lost. Hannibal was injured in battle and lost an eye to infection, yet he kept fighting—and winning! For 17 years Hannibal and his forces ravaged southern and central Italy with impunity. It got so bad that the Romans gave up engaging him in battle altogether.

The young Roman general Scipio had a different idea. Instead of attacking Hannibal directly, he led an army into Spain to take the Carthaginians in that land. After he successfully conquered Spain for Rome in 206 BCE, Scipio was elected consul (leader) of Rome at the age of 31. For Scipio, his next move was to meet the Carthaginian general in person.

Scipio raised a force of about 40,000 Roman troops and landed in Tunisia, ready for war with Hannibal. When the Carthaginians arrived on a plain near the town of Zama in 202

BCE, Hannibal had about an equal force, but he had a wily wildcard ... 80 war elephants.

Since the Carthaginians were famous for using war elephants, Scipio knew that his foe would have some at Zama, so he came prepared. He made sure that his front lines could withstand the initial shock of seeing the large, intimidating beasts charging by putting his veterans and those familiar with elephants at the front. Once the elephants did charge, Scipio then initiated the next part of his plan. He simply ordered his men to get out of the way!

Yes, it was as simple as that. Because elephants are wild animals, even domesticated ones can be difficult to control. Once the war elephants began their charge, if the enemy got out of the way, they would keep running for some distance. This allowed the Romans to close in with their superior cavalry numbers and slaughter the Carthaginians. Although Hannibal survived the battle, the Romans won the war and took over the Carthaginian Empire, making them the most powerful people in the Mediterranean world.

History is a funny thing sometimes. The Battle of Zama could have easily gone the other way, and if so, the Carthaginians would've become the dominant power in the ancient world. So much of our world would be different today if the Carthaginians had won. We may be using the Punic (the name of the Carthaginians' language) alphabet, our government would be based on the Carthaginian model, and our legal system and much of our science would be from Carthage, not Rome. So, you could say that the world we live in today is the result of the Romans getting out of the way of some elephants.

It's Not Slang, It's Creole

One of the major barriers that humans have encountered throughout history has been language. The language barrier is the first barrier, if you think about it—it prohibits people from communicating with each other, which in turn can prevent trade and other social exchanges.

Throughout human history, societies have come up with different methods to overcome the language barrier, with differing degrees of effectiveness and long-term results.

The most common way that people have beat the language barrier was by developing a *lingua franca*. A *lingua franca*, which means "French language" in Latin, is a dominant language that is spoken and/or written by the elites. It is the primary language of commerce, diplomacy, and other important activities during a particular period.

Akkadian was the *lingua franca* of the Bronze Age Near East, Chinese has been the *lingua franca* in different periods of Asian history, French was the *lingua franca* of the Western world in the 1700s, and many would argue that English is the *lingua franca* of the world today.

But not everyone has the time to learn a second language, and the reality is that, throughout most of human history, the majority of people couldn't even read and write in their native language. So, what did the average sailor or merchant do

44

when he had to deal with people who spoke another language? They developed what is known as a pidgin.

A pidgin is a simplified way for people who speak different languages to communicate and it works by people developing certain words and simple elements of language. Pidgins have existed since the dawn of humankind, but they became very common about 500 years ago when Europeans began exploring and colonizing the world. European sailors developed pidgins to communicate with non-European peoples.

It is important to know that pidgins are simple and are built around basic phrases and words—the development of complex syntax and verb conjugations is usually not part of a pidgin. Occasionally, though, pidgins become more complex and develop into a full-fledged language. These are then known as creole languages.

Most of the world's creole languages have disappeared, but Haitian Creole, simply known as kreyòl by native speakers, is the best known and most widely spoken creole language in the world. Based on French grammar of the 1700s, Haitian Creole borrows vocabulary and grammatical elements from Spanish, Portuguese, and several west African languages to create a language that is only vaguely related to modern French.

Throughout history, some have viewed creole languages as not proper languages, but today most linguists and philologists agree that creoles are true languages and not simply slang dialects.

Look for the Lights

Argentina is a South American nation that is known for its friendly people, laid back atmosphere, and scenic beauty. The capital city of Buenos Aires is a hip, happening, cosmopolitan locale, but if you're into more natural surroundings, there are plenty of nice beaches up and down the country's coastline.

The Patagonia region has attracted explorers for centuries and the Andes Mountains comprise the western spine of the nation, providing some of the best hiking and skiing in the southern hemisphere.

But if you're ever in the Calingasta Valley of the San Juan province, look out for some mysterious lights. You may not have to look for them at all because they always seem to find weary travelers.

The Calingasta Valley is a hot, arid region that lies in the foothills of the Andes Mountains. Apple orchards and vineyards dot the area, but it is mostly pretty desolate, which makes the high number of strange occurrences that have taken place there even stranger.

For decades, locals and visitors to the region have reported seeing strange balls of light that hover over hills, dry lake beds, and highways in the valley. The orbs often seem to move away when a person comes toward them but have also been reported to have followed and even chased travelers.

The orbs of light seem to operate with intelligence, which has led many to believe that they are otherworldly. But what world did they come from?

There has been no shortage of theories that have explained the origin or purpose of the Calingasta Valley lights. The more mundane theories hold that the lights are simply an optical illusion caused by a combination of the desert sands, heat, and travelers' imaginations. Others think that the lights have something to do with top-secret military experiments.

And then there are the more interesting theories. One story is that the lights are lanterns guiding lost travelers out of the desert and back to civilization. A related folk tale states that the lights are beacons leading to lost treasures, but whether they are benevolent or malevolent depends on the person telling the story. The more positive version states that the lights are there to help treasure hunters find lost gold and to bring it out of the valley successfully. Meanwhile, others think that the lights guide treasure hunters to a fortune that they'll never be able to claim!

Many are convinced that the Calingasta Valley lights are somehow related to other phenomena reported in nearby regions in Argentina. For instance, on July 19, 2008, the people of the town of Cachi in the Salta province reported seeing a UFO that was captured on film.

There have also been sightings of small, bipedal creatures roaming the Argentine foothills. Some locals claim that these creatures are magical imps that have been living in the region for centuries. As bizarre as all of this may sound, one thing is for sure—something strange is going on in northwestern Argentina!

Telekinesis or Parlor Trick?

Telekinesis is the supposed ability to move and/or change physical objects with psychic energy. When mysticism became a popular pastime for wealthy people in the late 1800s, men and women who claimed telekinetic powers traveled from city to city charging admission to see their wondrous acts. Of course, most of these psychics proved to be charlatans.

Although the vast majority of these professed psychics turned out to be frauds, you have to give them credit for being clever, ingenious, and industrious. Some of these fraudsters would use hairs and barely visible wires to make objects move and others would manipulate what was, at the time, the fairly new technology of photography to produce eerie images of objects seemingly floating in the air. Because so many of these psychic hoaxes were perpetuated in parlors of big homes, they became known as "parlor tricks."

Telekinesis was largely relegated to the fringes of society until Israeli Uri Geller began claiming that he could bend spoons, keys, and other metal objects with his mind. Geller underwent many tests/performances of his apparent ability and genuinely seemed to be the real deal ... until he was busted by notable stage magician James Randi and scientist Martin Gardner. The men proved that Geller was simply using a combination of stage props and sleight of hand to produce an entertaining yet fully fraudulent 20th-century parlor trick.

Still, many people insisted that there was something to the spoon bending trick. Seemingly normal people appeared to be able to bend spoons by placing their thumbs on the neck and applying minimal pressure. Since so many people have done this trick, it can't be a parlor trick, can it? Most psychiatrists and psychologists say that it is simply a case of "mind over matter." You are putting plenty of force on the neck of the spoon, you just don't realize it. Well, this may explain many of those cases; it can't, however, explain how young children and elderly people are also able to bend spoons with ease.

The fun thing about this is you can test it for yourself! Get a cheap spoon out of your drawer, put each of your thumbs on the neck of the spoon where the head begins, and concentrate on "seeing" the spoon bend. You may be surprised at the results.

Once you've bent your first spoon, you'll then have the personal experience to decide if it was the result of telekinetic power, a parlor trick, or mind over matter.

The Next One Could Turn Out All the Lights

You've no doubt heard about the "Big One," a high magnitude earthquake that is predicted to erupt on the San Andreas Fault Line on America's west coast, killing millions and making Las Vegas a coastal city. As we wait for the destruction of that killer earthquake to strike from below, maybe we should all be looking at the potential for even worse destruction from above.

The reality is that the entire advanced technological system that binds the world together—all of our coaxial cables, Internet, and cellphone infrastructure—rests on a very precarious base. One major jolt could wipe out the entire grid and put us all back into the 1800s, at least, but probably more like the 1500s. An earthquake could create massive localized damage to the grid, but a massive solar storm could destroy the grid worldwide.

So, what is a solar storm and why should we be worried? Without getting too much into the science, a solar storm is an eruption of energy on the Sun that sends flares outward to the Earth. Since the 1600s, when scientists first began observing the Sun's activities, they have noticed that it erupts in heightened activities for about ten-year periods, which they call solar cycles. We are currently in solar cycle 24, but it was solar cycle 10 that can give us an example of a potential worst-case scenario.

Solar cycle 10 began in 1855, but from September 1–2, 1859, it severely affected life throughout Earth. It became known as the Carrington Event, for the British scientist who first documented it, Richard Carrington. People living closer to the poles could see beautiful auroras and the flares were so bright that they lit up the sky at night. Most people thought it was a wonderful experience, but it did cause some problems.

The flares sent shocks through telegraph systems around the world, taking most of them offline. Thankfully for the world, the telegraph was still a fairly new technology in 1859 and the world wasn't yet dependent on it for communication. With that said, it still took years to repair most of the damaged lines.

You don't have to be a rocket scientist, or a solar flare scientist, to imagine the devastation that a Carrington Event could cause today. Scientists believe that we just narrowly missed a similar solar storm in 2012, but an 1859 magnitude storm could happen at any time. What will you do if a solar flare cuts off the lights?

The I-70 Killer

A cursory examination of serial killers reveals that they are truly a diverse lot. Some are driven for sadistic and sexual reasons, while others believe they are on a mission to rid the world of undesirables. Many serials killers meticulously plan every detail of their murders, but some kill out of convenience.

What drives one to become a serial killer is also a murky subject. Some of the best-known serial killers had truly awful upbringings, while others had seemingly normal childhoods. Perhaps the least studied aspect of serial killer culture is what makes them quit killing. There seems to be an idea that all serial killers have an insatiable desire to kill that can never be completely quenched and that they only stop when they are captured.

But is this always the case? Can a serial killer just decide that he's killed enough and go back to a normal life? This idea is often debated, with those who say some serial killers can stop pointing to the I-70 Killer as an example.

The I-70 Killer gunned down at least six people in the Midwest and Texas from 1992 to 1994. He was described as a younger-looking white male who could blend into just about any crowd. The authorities chasing the I-70 Killer believed that it was just a matter of time before he made a mistake and was caught. But then, just like that, he quit killing. What happened to the I-70 Killer?

It's believed that the I-70 Killer began his spree when he murdered 26-year-old Robin Fuldauer in a Payless ShoeSource store in Indianapolis, Indiana on April 8, 1992. It is believed that the killer went into the store just before closing, ushered Robin into the back at gunpoint, and then shot her to death. Robin was not sexually assaulted and only a small amount of money was taken.

The I-70 Killer struck four more times in April and May of that year in cities along the I-70 corridor in Kansas, Missouri, and Indiana. The method of operation and signature of the killer was almost always the same. Except for a double murder in Wichita, the victims were working alone and were almost always young and attractive. Although one man was murdered, the police believe he may have been mistaken for a woman due to his ponytail. The killer only took small amounts of money and he never sexually assaulted his victims.

The murders were quickly linked because the killer used the same .22 caliber pistol, but that did little to help the authorities. The killer was crafty enough not to leave any DNA or fingerprints at the scenes of his murders and he was only spotted very briefly on one occasion. The best the criminal profilers could come up with was that he lived somewhere in the Midwest, was in his 20s to 30s, and probably hated women.

The I-70 Killer may have then struck again in Texas in 1993, killing a woman, and then again in Texas in 1994, nearly killing another woman. The MO was the same in both of those cases.

The authorities did whatever they could to generate leads, even profiling the case on a season six episode of *Unsolved Mysteries*, but nothing substantial turned up. There were a couple of seemingly promising leads of other known killers potentially being the culprits, though those turned out to be dead ends.

So, what happened to the I-70 Killer? Some authorities believe that he may be doing time for another murder that doesn't fit the MO of the I-70 murders. Since he didn't leave behind any physical evidence in the I-70 murders, he remains unpunished for those killings. Another theory is that he is dead. The problem with that theory, though, is that he was relatively young when he was committing the murders and would now only be in his late 40s or 50s. And although he may be in prison for another murder—or murders—it is just as likely that he is living a free, normal life.

The more we learn about serial killers, the more we know that what makes them stop killing is just as complex as what triggers them to kill. The recently arrested Golden State Killer, Joseph James DeAngelo, and the Green River Killer, Gary Ridgway, are two perfect examples of serial killers blending into society. Both of those men had families, careers (DeAngelo was a former cop), and were described as good neighbors. Perhaps most importantly, DeAngelo and Ridgway both stopped killing after many years. For whatever reasons, they seemed to have grown tired of killing.

It is just as likely that the I-70 Killer simply grew tired of killing and quit, as he was to have been caught for another murder or dead. The I-70 Killer may have killed for the thrill and then stopped when his bloodlust was sated, or he may have been conducting a sick experiment to prove to himself he could get away with it. Whatever the case, there is a good chance that the I-70 Killer is living near one of you reading this.

Bookworms

You've no doubt heard the word "bookworm" at some point in your life, and since you're now reading this piece of literature, there is a good chance you are a bibliophile and have been called one at some point. You may also know that there is a type of insect known as a bookworm that feasts on the glue in book bindings. So, which of these terms came first, and are they even related?

Research has traced the earliest use of the term bookworm back to 1500s England. It meant pretty much the same thing then as it does today—a person who spends a lot of time buried in books. But unlike today, where the term is seen as cute or as a compliment of someone's intellectual abilities, it was a pejorative in Renaissance England.

A worm was one of the greatest insults you could call someone because they were considered such lowly creatures. A man who only dedicated himself to reading was viewed as rather unmanly and not very reliable. Eventually, though, by the late 1800s, the term came to take on a more positive, or at least playful, meaning.

The earliest known reference to actual insects that infest old books is from the 1700s. Although there are several species of insects that can infest old books, the Psocoptera is the order to which most of the species known generally as booklice or bookworms belong.

Bookworms are scavengers that feed on and lay eggs in the glue in book bindings of old, usually neglected books. Bookworms don't resemble worms in any way, so the reason they became known as such probably goes back to the original term.

The negative connotation of bookworm had already been around for a while and so had the insects that infested old books, but because the term for bibliophiles was well-known, it began to be applied to the insect. After all, it's a lot easier to say that bookworms, not Psocoptera, have infested a book, right?

What Happened to Butch Cassidy and the Sundance Kid?

Robert LeRoy Parker, better known as Butch Cassidy, and his trusted partner, Harry Alonzo Longabaugh, the Sundance Kid, were the last of America's Old West outlaws. From 1889 into the early 1900s, Butch, Sundance, and their gang—known as The Wild Bunch—traversed the western states and territories, robbing banks and trains, and earning themselves a nice bit of loot and sizable reputations in the process.

But both the United States and the world were changing very quickly then. A web of telegraph and railroad lines had spanned out across the nation connecting even some of the most remote parts of the West. Most Americans saw the days of the Wild West as over and wanted the government to reign in the few remaining outlaws. Butch and Sundance saw the writing on the wall.

By 1901, the Wild Bunch had earned quite a reputation; they were wanted in several states for robbery. Although they attempted to negotiate for amnesty with the governor of Utah, they were wanted in multiple states and, worse for them, the railroad companies had sent the private Pinkerton Detective Agency after them.

Butch and Sundance knew it was time to leave the country, so in February 1901—along with Sundance's girlfriend Etta

Place—they boarded a ship bound for Argentina. Because of Argentina's pro-European immigration policy at the time, the trio was able to blend into greater Argentine society.

The pair used their earnings from robberies in the United States to buy a sizable ranch in the foothills of the Andes Mountains in the Patagonia region in southern Argentina. For a time, it looked like the former outlaws would live out their lives peacefully. But as the saying goes, a leopard can't change its spots.

I guess Patagonia reminded the pair too much of the western U.S. The wide-open space, free-roaming cattle, and isolated towns proved to be too much of a temptation for the bandits. They began robbing rural banks in Argentina in 1905 and were eventually chased north into Bolivia. The pair went straight again for a while when they found work as security guards in a Bolivian mine. Needless to say, background checks weren't very thorough back then!

Once again, the lure of easy riches and the thrill of a robbery was just too much for Butch and Sundance. After learning how the mines moved their payrolls, the duo decided to rob the payroll of a mine in a neighboring town on November 3, 1908. The robbery went off well, but they made a rookie mistake by taking one of the company's branded mules.

The Bolivian Army quickly tracked down the American outlaws, cornering and supposedly killing them on November 7, 1908. I say "supposedly" because this is where the legend of Butch Cassidy and the Sundance Kid goes to the next level.

The Bolivian Army's account is that the two men began shooting at them when they arrived, killing one soldier. The soldiers opened fire for several hours and then went into the house the next day. Both men had several gunshot wounds and it appeared that Butch had possibly shot Sundance as a mercy killing and then shot himself in the head.

Since the Bolivian authorities didn't know who the men were at the time, other than a couple of Americans, they were never positively identified and were buried in anonymous graves in a San Vicente, Bolivia cemetery. News of the deaths eventually filtered back to the United States, making Butch Cassidy and the Sundance Kid the last of the West's great outlaws to die in the line of action … or did they?

Beginning in the 1960s, rumors that the men had survived the shootout in Bolivia began circulating. Butch especially was the subject of some pretty detailed stories about how he returned to the U.S. in the 1920s. And the stories were told by some fairly credible sources.

Josie Bassett, one of Butch's former lovers from his Wild Bunch days, said that he returned in the 1920s to visit friends and family in Utah before retiring to Nevada where he later died. Cassidy's sister, Lulu Parker Betenson, also claimed that he returned to the United States and retired to Washington state, dying there in the 1930s. Although far fewer in occurrence, there were also claims that the Sundance Kid returned to his home in Utah.

Etta Place's fate is also a mystery of history. It's known that she left Butch and Sundance in 1906 and returned to the United States, but what she did after that is unknown. Some say that she became a brothel madam, while others believe she married and lived out her life as a law-abiding citizen. One other theory is that she never left Sundance, as a woman matching her description attempted to get a death certificate for Sundance in Bolivia.

Today, Butch Cassidy and the Sundance Kid are remembered as anti-heroes who took on the system and came out on top, at least for a while. Since they are remembered fondly, many like to believe that they survived the shootout with the Bolivian Army and made their way back to the United States. The chances are that their bodies were placed in those unmarked graves in San Vicente, Bolivia, but it is much more romantic to think that they got away and were able to retire in style.

Your Choice of Execution

Capital punishment is a hot button issue. Those opposed to it argue it is a violation of the U.S. Constitution's Eighth Amendment, which prohibits "cruel and unusual punishment."

Those in favor of capital punishment point out that executions were routinely performed when the Constitution was written and that the only people executed are the worst of the worst killers. Anti-death penalty activists also argue that innocent people can be executed, while pro-death penalty advocates argue that there is no proof anyone innocent has ever been executed.

The reality is that the United States is pretty much alone among industrialized countries regarding capital punishment; it is only one of 55 countries that regularly uses the death penalty for criminals, along with the likes of China, Iran, Egypt and, perhaps somewhat surprisingly, Japan.

But Americans also like to be unique and trendsetters and their application of the death penalty is no different. Whereas most countries have only one method of execution, the United States has multiple, which is partly due to the nature of the U.S.'s federal government system but also due to other considerations.

A capital crime in the United States—the worst crime under the law and therefore capable of being punished by execution—is murder. Murders are usually prosecuted under state law. Twenty-eight U.S. states currently have the death penalty, and all decide the method according to their state legislatures.

The gas chamber was the main method used in California for several years, but the electric chair has been the most common method. Hanging used to be the method in Washington and Delaware, while Utah uses a firing squad.

But the anti-death penalty forces had plenty of resources and were able to mount successful legal challenges to different execution methods, so most of the states turned to the lethal injection. Lethal injection has also been legally challenged due to some botched executions, but it remains the de facto execution method in every state.

In some states—primarily in the polite South—the condemned are offered a choice of execution methods. Alabama, Florida, Kentucky, South Carolina, Tennessee, and Virginia are nice enough to provide some condemned inmates the choice of the electric chair, while California and Arizona have the gas chamber as an alternative. Not surprisingly, no one is yet to pick the gas chamber.

In Utah, Mississippi, and Oklahoma, some inmates have the choice of going out like a hero in front of a firing squad. I say "some inmates" because in Arizona, Kentucky, Tennessee, and Utah the alternative form of execution is only offered to those convicted before a certain date. In all of the states with alternative methods, the other methods can also be used if lethal injection is ruled unconstitutional or the prison is unable to get the drugs and chemicals needed for the execution.

The Face on Mars

When the NASA *Viking 1* probe passed by Mars on July 25, 1976, it became the first human spacecraft to make it to and observe the Red Planet. It was truly a monumental step forward in human development.

Many thought that the probe would be the beginning of human colonization on Mars, hopefully helping alleviate Earthly problems such as overpopulation, poverty, and hunger in the process.

But many people were anxious to see what secrets may lie on the surface of the dusty planet. Perhaps life existed on Mars in some form, or maybe an advanced civilization once called the planet its home?

Those who believed that Mars held the secrets of life beyond Earth felt justified when photos the *Viking 1* took were released to the public. Most of the pictures just showed a mountainous region of Mars known as Cydonia, but almost lost among all the photos were two that caught some people's eyes. *Surely it can't be,* thought experts. Yet there it was … it was a face on the surface of Mars!

For 20 years the photos of the "Face on Mars," as it became known, were studied by experts and conspiracy theorists alike. The more the *Viking 1* pictures were examined, the more interesting things on the planet's surface people began to see.

In addition to the Face, people began claiming to see pyramids and other structures that looked humanmade.

Could there have been an ancient civilization on Mars that predated anything on Earth by thousands of years?

Possible, but not likely. Advances in photo technology allowed experts to view higher resolution images of the Face, which show that it is just a mountain with some curious yet natural ridges. And the pyramids on Mars? Well, those are just regular mountains, but since people were already looking for something humanmade due to the "Face on Mars," they saw pyramids instead of mountains.

The phenomenon of people seeing faces or familiar objects, rather than the actual object—such as the Face on Mars or mountains on Mars as pyramids—is known as pareidolia. For now, experts believe that pareidolia explains the Face on Mars and any other strange-looking structure on Mars. This sounds like a reasonable, logical explanation to most people, but even the most skeptical people must have a small part that still wonders.

We'll never know for sure if Martians built an advanced civilization unless we go there, but unfortunately for us, NASA currently has no plans to send a manned expedition to Mars.

The Most Haunted House in America

If you're ever in Cleveland, Ohio, go to the Ohio City neighborhood and take a look at the house at 4308 Franklin Boulevard ... or don't. It looks like an imposing castle in the middle of the industrial city, which is how it got its nickname, Franklin Castle.

It's what's inside, however, that earned the house its reputation as the most haunted house in America. The house was originally owned by a wealthy German immigrant named Hannes Tiedemann, who had the mansion built in the 1880s. Through some unfortunate accidents and fate, and some would say murder, five members of the Tiedemann family died there in its first few years of existence. According to those who have visited Franklin Castle, the dead Tiedemanns never left.

The first of the Tiedemann clan to die was Hannes and his wife Louise's 15-year-old daughter Emma, in 1891 from diabetes. Although she was young and afflicted with what is today a very controllable disease, medicine in the 1800s wasn't what it is today, so her death was not seen as particularly unusual. Not long after Emma died, Hannes' mother Wiebeka died in the home. Wiebeka was old, so her death didn't raise many eyebrows either. But then three more of the Tiedemann children died and Louise herself died later.

But the story doesn't end here. How could it? As members of the Tiedemann family were dropping dead left and right, Hannes began making additions to the mansion, including new staircases and supposedly hidden rooms. By the time Hannes sold the house in 1896, he was rumored to have murdered a mistress and at least one family member other than his daughters.

Tiedemann sold the home to a brewing company and it also later served as a headquarters for a German–American cultural organization, but its legacy of death always followed. It was owned by the German Socialist Party during World War I and may have been the scene of an anti-German mass murder. Rumor has it that a man upset about Germany's actions in World War I went in there with a machine gun and gunned a few people down.

Over the years, visitors and occupants of Franklin Castle have reported numerous apparitions, objects moving on their own, cold spots throughout the house, the sound of children crying, and just a general feeling of dread. Human bones were even found in a closet in 1975, although most people think it was part of a hoax by the owner at the time to cash in on the legend. One owner even claimed that his children were playing with ghosts when he wasn't around!

Franklin Castle has remained primarily vacant since the mid-1980s, although it has had plenty of different owners. In 2012, it was reported that Franklin Castle was being converted into apartments, but that hasn't happened. It's as if the house truly is cursed.

Franklin Castle has been featured on paranormal television shows *Paranormal Lockdown* and *Ghost Adventures*, adding to the house's allure and claim to be the most haunted in

America. One thing is for sure, those who have been inside Franklin Castle will swear that it is haunted.

Skiing Downunder, Mate

Millions of people around the world love to ski as a pastime. Some of the more hardcore skiers—and those with some money—take trips to the Swiss Alps, Colorado, and British Colombia, just to name three of the more popular spots. Those wanting to see more exotic slopes can go to Japan, Chile, or Argentina … or Australia. Yes, if you want a really unique skiing vacation, you can hit the slopes Downunder. Just remember, if you want to try it, the best time to go is in the middle of July because that is the dead of winter in Australia.

When you think of Australia, alpine ski slopes are not the first things that come to mind. It is probably one of the last, if it comes to mind at all. Beaches, the Outback, kangaroos, and koalas are what most people associate with Australia. However, if you're down there during summer in the Northern Hemisphere, which is winter in the Southern Hemisphere, you may want to check out one of the many ski resorts.

Nearly all of the skiing in Australia is done in the southeastern corner of the country in a swath of pristine land known as the Australian Alps National Parks and Reserves, which is located in parts of the states of Victoria and New South Wales, and the Australian Capital Territory. The specific mountain range where most of the ski resorts are is known as the Snowy Mountains (or the Snowies).

The highest peaks in the Snowy Mountains get above 7,000 feet, which is enough for snow in the winter months of June through September. It's not high enough, however, for the snow to stay year-round.

So, if you ever vacation in Australia in the summer and you get tired of the beaches and desert, the Snowy Mountains are always there for a Southern Hemisphere skiing adventure.

Thermodynamic Equilibrium

You've no doubt made ice cubes at some point and probably also watched as some of those cubes melted. You've probably also boiled water, turning part of it into a gas. However, have you ever modified a substance so that it is liquid, solid, and gas *at the same time*? If you have, then you've achieved what is known as "triple point" or thermodynamic equilibrium.

The term triple point was first coined by British scientist James Thomson (1822–1892) to describe the state at which a substance is solid, liquid, *and* gas. James' younger brother William later used knowledge of triple point to construct the kelvin scale.

All of this may sound like some ultra-nerdy material, but it is quite easy to understand. Every substance has a triple point, though it is dependent on temperature *and* pressure. For instance, the triple point of water is 32 °F (freezing), but a partial vapor pressure of 611.657 pascals is required to bring the water to all three states. Minor variations can change the water to ice or gas, or back to liquid. Some elements and substances have pretty extreme triple points compared to water. Carbon has a triple point of a whopping 8,117 °F and 10,132 pascals. On the other end, Helium-4 has a triple point of -455 F° 30 pascals.

So, you're probably wondering, "All of this is interesting to know, but does knowing it have any practical benefit?" Well, one notable instance when triple point was used was when NASA's Mariner 9 probe flew over Mars in 1972. Since Mars has no liquid surface water, the probe used triple point to determine what the sea levels would be on Mars, although today NASA uses laser altimetry.

If you're the kind of person who likes to conduct your own science experiments, triple point can be kind of fun. All you need is the ability to freeze, melt, and boil whatever substance you are attempting to bring to triple point. Just remember to be careful.

Hollow Earth Theory

In recent years, there's been a reemergence of people who subscribe to the Flat Earth theory. It's just as it sounds: the Earth is flat, or not a sphere, and we've been misled to believe otherwise. Flat Earth proponents range in their thinking as to how and why people stopped believing the Earth was flat.

Many believe that humanity became arrogant, yet naively so, with its so-called scientific knowledge, which eventually led to the erroneous belief that the Earth is a sphere. Others think that a conscious conspiracy is in place by the world's leaders and scientific community to keep knowledge of the Earth's flat nature a secret, for whatever reason.

The reality is that the educated Greeks knew the Earth was a sphere in the 5th century BCE and very few educated people in Columbus' time, or mariners for that matter, believed the Earth was flat. But what about it being hollow?

The Hollow Earth theory, as it is sometimes called, is just as old as the Flat Earth theory and was believed by scientists for a much longer period. Even after modern science proved that the Earth was much larger than formerly believed, and for the most part solid, fiction about Hollow Earth and esoteric theories based on it persisted.

Many premodern peoples had myths and stories about subterranean worlds that were as advanced, if not more so, than their own. In the Sumerian *Epic of Gilgamesh*, the hero Gilgamesh travels to a world beneath the surface of the Earth to learn the secrets of life.

Similarly, according to the Tibetan Buddhist tradition, the city of Shambhala was located somewhere within the Earth. The ancient Greeks, Vikings, and different American Indian tribes also had legends about civilizations and races, both benevolent and malevolent, living underground.

Even after these ancient religious ideas were replaced with the universal religions of Christianity and Islam, the notion that the Earth is hollow, or partially hollow, and potentially home to different intelligent races, was for the most part accepted.

The Hollow Earth theory was bolstered by English scientist Edmond Halley (1656–1742) in 1692. Now, Halley was no crackpot; he's the guy that Halley's Comet is named after. But his theory about the Earth is strange considering what we know today.

Halley believed that the Earth's core was an empty, 500-mile wide circle that was surrounded by a concentric circle, which was also surrounded by a circle. He also believed that there was a regular atmosphere inside the Earth and that there was a strong possibility that intelligent beings existed in the core. The scientific community, and therefore mainstream society, bought Halley's theory. After all, he was a prominent scientist, so he couldn't be wrong, right?

Well, not everyone agreed with the Hollow Earth theory and some were quite vocal about it, but it was another English scientist, Charles Hutton (1737–1823), who ultimately proved Halley wrong. In a 1774 experiment known as the Schiehallion experiment, Hutton proved the Earth's density.

However, this did not put an end to the idea of the Hollow Earth.

The late 1800s saw the rise of mysticism and esoteric ideas throughout much of the West, including the pseudo-religion of Theosophy in the United States. Theosophy was led by a mystic named Helena Blavatsky who believed in many non-conventional ideas, one of which was the idea of Hollow Earth. But the Theosophy Hollow Earth idea was a bit different. The new Hollow Earth theory held that the Earth is convex, and the Sun and the nighttime sky are inside the Earth.

This version of the Hollow Earth theory continued to be advanced and was believed by some of the mystics in the Nazi Party. Heinrich Himmler and many of his mystic pals in the SS believed the Hollow Earth theory and thought that there were two entrances to the subterranean world: one in the North Pole and one in the South Pole.

There are even rumors that the SS conducted expeditions to find one or both of the entrances, although that has never been proven.

After World War II, the Hollow Earth theory continued to be promoted by neo-fascist philosophers such as Chilean Miguel Serrano (1917–2009), but for the most part, it was relegated to fiction. Numerous books, movies, and television shows have plots that revolve around the Earth being hollow, or partially hollow, and full of amazing creatures and civilizations. Jules Verne's 1864 book *Journey to the Center of the Earth* set off the craze, but others followed suit, including the notoriously bad 1956 Z-film, *The Mole People*.

There will no doubt be more films made with Hollow Earth themes in the future and some people continue to follow some of the esoteric beliefs about the convex Earth.

This may seem strange to most of us, but ask yourself: "What's cooler and more interesting, the idea that the Earth may be hollow and filled with subterranean civilizations, or that it is flat?" I think almost all of you reading this will answer Hollow Earth!

The Ghost Ship Warehouse Fire

On the night of December 2, 2016, an often-overlooked warehouse in the Fruitvale neighborhood of Oakland, California went up in flames. As firetrucks raced to put out the fire, they were also tasked with rescuing more than 100 people inside the warehouse, which turned out to be an unlicensed music club known as the Ghost Ship.

Thirty-six people lost their lives in the Ghost Ship fire, making it the deadliest in California since the 1906 fires that followed an earthquake. Once the police and media began investigating the Ghost Ship and the people involved, a bizarre scene quickly unfolded.

Derick Almena began leasing the building from owner Chor Ng in 2013. He told Ng that they were going to turn the building into an artist's collective called the Ghost Ship that would be open 24 hours to members. In reality, Almena was just looking to make a few quick bucks. He moved his wife and children into the building and quickly began subleasing the building to hipsters and other young urbanites trying to escape from San Francisco's high rents while still staying in the Bay Area.

Almena lived on the second floor with his family, while the first floor consisted of artist spaces and living areas. The first-floor areas were haphazardly divided by makeshift walls made of cardboard and whatever else was laying around. Electrical power was channeled to the spaces through wiring that was substandard at best. Paper, plastic, and other flammable materials were regularly strewn about the Ghost Ship, there were only two exits from the building, and there were no fire alarms. It was an accident waiting to happen, but instead of getting those things fixed, Almena decided to start hosting concerts and raves.

The late-night concerts and raves brought Almena a new revenue source and increased his and the Ghost Ship's reputation among the hipsters and artists of the Bay Area. It was viewed and even advertised by Almena as a primitive and primordial place where artists could affordably live and express themselves. It was also promoted as a place where you could catch cutting-edge music. But even in ultra-liberal Oakland, not everyone was happy with the Ghost Ship.

Ng was fined and warned repeatedly for not properly maintaining the building and for Almena operating business and residential spaces there when it was only zoned for industrial. Not to mention that the skulls and other bizarre images painted on the outside of its walls tended to creep locals out. These death motifs that were scattered throughout the Ghost Ship turned out to be a harbinger of what was to come.

All 36 of the Ghost Ship victims died of smoke inhalation, which authorities say possibly could have been avoided if the building was properly ventilated, had more exits, and the interior wasn't such a haphazard maze. Investigations by local and federal authorities revealed that the fire began due to faulty wiring and was exacerbated by all the wood, plastic, and junk throughout the building. The Ghost Ship was a tragedy waiting to happen.

Almena and his assistant, Max Harris, were charged with involuntary manslaughter in 2018 and held in the Alameda County Jail awaiting trial. In September 2019, Harris was acquitted of all charges and freed, while the jury in Almena's case deadlocked so he was remanded back to jail to await a new trial.

In a new twist to what is already a very strange case, Almena was released from jail in April 2020 due to the coronavirus. He still faces the prospect of another trial, but the way things have gone, the charges may very well be dropped. Whatever happens, there's sure to be at least one more strange turn in the case of the Oakland Ghost Ship.

Is That Satan Talking?

If you were around in the 1980s in the United States, especially if you were a teenager, then surely you remember the Satanic Panic. Investigative news shows like *60 Minutes* and "journalists" such as Geraldo Rivera conducted "in-depth" reports on the murky Satanic underbelly of America.

According to these reports, the Satanists had infiltrated most elements of American society and were particularly trying to capture the hearts and minds of American children.

Anti-Satanist experts, who were usually "concerned mothers," argued that Satanism could be seen in toys such as He-Man and the Masters of the Universe and games like Dungeons and Dragons. If parents didn't do something about it, they said, they risked losing their children to cold vices of the Satanic conspiracy. But the anti-Satanist crusaders reserved most of their attention for rock and heavy metal bands.

Just as their parents had attacked Elvis and the Beatles in the 1950s and '60s, parents in the 1980s attacked Ozzy Osbourne, Slayer, and Mötley Crüe.

Many of the bands played the hysteria up by incorporating the occult and Satanism into their imagery for effect, but the anti-Satanist groups claimed that their true message—their evil and nefarious message—could only be heard if you listened to their songs very closely … or backward.

So began the great backmasking controversy of the 1980s, which was but a chapter in the greater Satanic Panic. Backmasking is the term for when a word or words are recorded backward on a track, so they are masked when played forward. Several bands have been accused of employing backmasking in their hit songs.

"Highway to Heaven" by Led Zeppelin is said to say "My sweet Satan" when played backward and the Styx song "Snowblind" sounds as if the band says "Satan moves through our voices" when played backward.

The original backmasked track was "Revolution 9" by the Beatles, where John Lennon is thought to be saying "Paul is Dead." AC/DC, Rush, and Queen were also accused of promoting Satanism through backmasked songs, although it now appears more likely that it was either an accident those songs revealed Satanic messages or they never did and only sound that way because that was what people were hoping or trying to hear.

By the early 1990s, the Satanic Panic had subsided and so too did the backmasking controversy. But as digital files have become the preferred media to consume music, more and more people are listening to their music to find potential backmasking tracks. So, go through some of your favorite MP3s and play them backward. You might hear a message from the devil.

Off with Their Heads!

In our earlier discussion about capital punishment in the United States, it was revealed that some murderous American criminals have a final choice before their lights are put out. This may seem unfair to some, but it should be remembered that the condemned don't have the choice of just any execution method. They can't choose the guillotine which, as scary as it looks, would probably be the quickest and cleanest method of execution. But you would have to find someone to sew your head back on if you want an open casket.

A guillotine is an execution device that consists of a frame that is about eight feet tall, consisting of two upright posts and a crossbeam at the top. Each post has a track that allows an oblique-edged blade to slide down it quickly when it is released by the executioner, who holds it in place with a rope. The condemned was placed prone on the bottom of the frame with their arms tied behind their back. The condemned then has their head placed in a stock and the executioner lets the blade fall and, as they say in France, voila!

The guillotine may seem like an ancient, or at least medieval, method of execution, but it has a very short history. It came into use as a *reaction* to medieval execution methods. Various versions of the guillotine were in use throughout Europe in the late Middle Ages and early Modern Period, but the most commonly used execution methods were usually painful public spectacles that mixed torture with execution. The breaking wheel was a device on which the condemned would be placed, stretched, and beaten over a long period until they finally died.

Death by fire was also a common form of execution, although it was usually reserved for heretics and those accused of sorcery and witchcraft. Other popular forms of execution included disembowelment, hanging, chopping off the head (it often took multiple whacks), and quartering. In case you're wondering what the last method entailed, it was when a criminal's legs and arms would be tied to four horses that would then run in opposite directions. The horses often went at different speeds, leaving a mangled mess of a criminal who was still alive, sometimes for minutes after the quartering.

When the Enlightenment swept over Europe in the 1700s, people's views on execution and crime and punishment began to change. Although most still believed that certain criminals should be executed, the idea that they should be tortured fell out of favor. People believed that it was more humane to kill the criminal as quickly and as painlessly as possible.

Joseph-Ignace Guillotin was a French doctor who was opposed to the death penalty on principle but familiar with methods whereby the condemned person's head was chopped off quickly. In 1789, he brought the execution method to the King of France, and by 1792, it was the only method used in France, where it became known as the guillotine.

The guillotine quickly saw plenty of action in France during the French Revolution (1789–1799), particularly during the phase of the revolution known as the Reign of Terror (1793–1794). It was during the Reign of Terror that thousands of nobles, church officials, and those generally opposed to the

French Revolution were executed by guillotine. Queen Marie Antoinette is famously quoted as saying "let them eat cake," about the common folk (although many historians believe that she never said that), but the revolutionaries responded by saying "off with her head," which they did on October 16, 1793.

Executions were usually public affairs, as the revolutionaries found them a good way to raise the morale of the people and to stoke their hatred against the elite. The executioner would often show the severed head to the crowd, who would be amazed by the deceased's still seemingly animated face. Of course, the person was dead; the facial movements were the result of residual nerves.

The Reign of Terror eventually fizzled out when nearly all the elites of France lost their heads. The situation opened the way for Napoleon Bonaparte to come to power, and although as a military man he often executed his enemies via firing squad, he continued to employ the guillotine for civilians. As France changed governments numerous times throughout the 1800s, the guillotine was one of the constants. By the 1900s, the guillotine became so much a part of French identity that people all over the world associated the execution method exclusively with France.

But times change and after World War II all of the nations of Western Europe began to ban execution as a form of criminal punishment. France performed its last execution by guillotine in 1977 and officially banned execution in 1981. Today, some older French citizens look back at the use of the guillotine with nostalgia, kind of as a symbol of a better time. Many of those citizens would bring back its use if they could, but under current European Union laws, execution is banned as a form of criminal punishment, so it doesn't look like legal head-chopping will come back in France anytime soon. If France leaves the European Union, however...

What Are Those Mounds?

If you've ever been to rural parts of the southeastern United States, rural areas of New Mexico, Arizona, or southern California, you may have noticed large dirt mounds, sometimes a foot high and even wider, that look somewhat out of place.

Chances are you probably also forgot about the mounds and went about your business. But if you would have taken a closer look, you'd have seen a whole world within those mounds. You would have seen workers of the ant genus Solenopsis building the mounds, just as humans would build skyscrapers.

If you ever do get close to one of those mounds, just make sure not to touch it because the ants that build them are more commonly known as Red Imported Fire Ants (RIFA). They're called fire ants because their bite emits a toxin that produces a painful, burning sensation.

There are several different RIFAs from the genus Solenopsis, but the ones in the southern United States originated in south-central South America. They are believed to have entered the United States in Alabama during the 1930s after hitching a ride on a ship from Argentina. Before too long, they were living throughout many states below the Mason–Dixon Line.

It was immediately clear that fire ants were an invasive species, destroying other ant species and insects as they made their way north. Once a fire ant colony decides to move into a new area, there is little that the other species can do. The fire ant invasion begins when the colony unleashes its army of 250,000 worker ants. The worker ants attack their enemies by biting for a grip and then injecting the venom from their stomach.

Fire ants are also extremely tough creatures. They don't hibernate, which allows them to stay active in the winter months, although once they get north of the Mason–Dixon Line they tend to die off in significant numbers. Fire ants thrive on hot temperatures, have effectively resisted most pesticides, and are quite adaptable when it comes to finding a place to live.

Although the large mounds found in rural areas are quite a sight, most fire ant colonies in suburban and urban settings are more nondescript. Fire ants will hide their colonies in populated areas under stairwells, in backyards, and just about anywhere else where they can conduct their industrious business.

If you happen to come across one of their urban colonies, you'll no doubt know about it! The painful stings will be a reminder that humans are not the only predator in the city. Fire ants are known to kill birds and even small mammals, but don't worry; humans aren't on their menu.

Despite alarming reports in the 1960s and '70s that fire ants would inundate the United States, causing mass casualties, few deaths have been reported. Enough bites can cause anaphylactic shock and death, so the elderly and the sick should avoid fire ants at all costs.

Fire ants may not be taking over the country, but if you live in the southern United States, you should exercise a little extra caution when you are somewhere they may live.

They Call It "Keistering"

No matter the country, prisons are bad places. Sure, prisons in some countries are more violent and overall worse than in other countries, but the joint is a place you never want to end up, no matter where you are. If you do happen to find yourself in the clink, you'll be stripped of pretty much all your rights and freedoms, separated from your loved ones and, of course, surrounded by sociopaths waiting for you to show any sign of weakness.

Many who are sentenced to extended stays courtesy of their state or federal government try to make the best of things by recreating their lives before prison. Some of these people find girlfriends and boyfriends behind bars, while others focus their energies on procuring substances they once enjoyed on the streets, namely drugs and alcohol. So, how do inmates get their favorite mind-altering drugs and other items behind bars?

Well, when it comes to booze, enterprising inmates have developed plenty of ways to make it themselves. Called "pruno" or "hooch," prison wine tastes awful, but it is known to be very powerful. Most prison-grade pruno is made from three simple ingredients: fruit, sugar, and bread. Inmates get the first ingredient by squeezing oranges from the kitchen or, if they are lucky, they can purchase pure fruit juice from the commissary.

Sugar cubes are available for purchase from most commissaries and bread can either be taken from the chow hall or some yeast can be purchased from an inmate who works in the kitchen.

A little water can be added for volume and then the concoction is sealed in a plastic container or bag. The mix is "breathed" occasionally, and within days, a batch is ready that can get several inmates drunk! But if your tastes go beyond booze and into more illicit drugs, then you'll have to be a bit more creative.

In many prisons, guards and civilian staff are often bribed by influential inmates and gang leaders to smuggle drugs into the facilities. The gangs then sell the drugs to other inmates, but there are, of course, other ways to smuggle stuff.

One of the most common ways that inmates have been able to get drugs into prisons is during visits. The process takes place when a visitor slips small balloons full of drugs to an inmate during a visit, who then either swallows the balloons or puts them in their rectum or vagina in what is known as "keistering." Yes, I'm sure you can guess the etymology of that term!

Keistering is common in prisons throughout the world and was even part of a joke in the movie *Pulp Fiction*, where a character explained how he keistered a precious memento while a prisoner of war in Vietnam. Inmates are known to keister not only drugs but also personal information and gang communication as well as homemade shanks.

Needless to say, keistering occasionally results in problems and the hospitalization of inmates trying to carry items that way. Okay, I know what you're thinking: what about the big items?

Cell phones have become more common in American prisons, usually smuggled in by guards and civilian employees, but items much bigger than that are rare or unheard of. The movies present an image that a person with enough influence or money can get anything they want in an American prison, but that simply isn't true. But in some other countries...

Prisons in many developing countries, especially Latin America, operate by different rules than in the industrialized world. In many of these countries, there's no need to keister items because prisons are just there to keep the inmates separated from society. Once the gates close, the inmate gangs control what happens on the inside with drugs and sex work—sometimes even with female sex workers in male prisons—being conducted openly. Gang wars are common, and it is not unheard of for the inmates to use guns.

In December 2019, a gang war broke out in the notorious La Joyita prison in Panama that left 14 inmates dead. When the smoke finally cleared—literally—officials seized three AK-47 assault rifles and five handguns.

The shootout grabbed headlines around the world, forcing Panama President Laurentino Cortizo to make a statement: "These firearms didn't fall out of the sky, there was obviously some type of cooperation there for firearms to be brought in." Um, you think so, Laurentino?

Did You Hear That Color?

When you listen to music, do you see different colors accompanying each note? Do you associate a specific color with certain numbers and letters? Have you ever tasted a word? If you've ever experienced any of these sensations, then you may have the rare neurological condition known as synesthesia. Notice, though, that I didn't call it a disorder because the overwhelming majority of people who have this aren't bothered by it at all and some even consider it a gift.

Little is known about synesthesia other than that its origins are from somewhere in the brain and that those who have it report having it their entire lives—they are born with it and it stays with them until death. About 1% to 4% of the population has synesthesia, but the exact numbers aren't known for a couple of reasons.

First, many people who have it aren't even aware that it is a condition until they are adults, so they never report it. Second, since synesthesia does not usually hinder a person's ability to lead a productive life, those with the condition often see no need to tell anyone. Also, there is no medication for synesthesia and the medical community doesn't consider it a disorder.

If you think you're a synesthete, don't worry; you're in good company! Many top musicians, actors, and scientists have been reported to have synesthesia, including Billy Joel, Lorde, Marilyn Monroe, and Vincent Van Gogh.

They Let Him Out of Prison

Most people think that the U.S. has the market cornered on serial killers, and although in terms of known cases that may be true, it isn't necessarily so when it comes to the most prolific serial killer in history. No, that honor would go to Colombian national Pedro Alonzo López, who is known to have raped and murdered at least 110 girls and women, but it is believed his kill count is probably closer to 300. What makes this case even more interesting is that he was released from prison.

Yes, you read that correctly. López, or the "Monster of the Andes" as he is known, was released after serving only 14 years behind bars. So, how did López become perhaps the worst serial killer in history and find freedom?

López's story began when he was born in the town of Santa Isabel, Colombia on October 8, 1948. Things started badly for López before he was even born—his father died in political violence and so his mother turned to sex work to feed her large family. By the age of ten, López was living on the streets of Bogotá, Colombia, committing petty crimes and doing drugs. Life on the streets left López vulnerable to abuse, which he repeatedly suffered. He also later claimed that he was sexually abused by a teacher at an orphanage, further serving to alienate him from society.

López eventually became a career criminal, landing in an adult prison for auto theft when he was still a teen. While in prison, the abuse continued when López was raped by several other inmates. But it was while he was in prison that López decided to quit being a victim. He murdered two of his attackers in retaliation and immediately went from being the prey to predator.

After being released from prison, López made a conscious decision to indulge his dark side. Based on his own experiences, López decided to target young girls whom he believed would be considered expendable. López traveled extensively throughout the Andean nations of Peru and Ecuador in the 1970s, targeting girls in isolated indigenous communities.

López survived a brush with angry locals and the law when he attempted to abduct a nine-year-old girl. The girl's community initially planned to bury López alive but eventually turned him over to the Peruvian police. The Peruvian authorities only deported López back to his native Colombia, allowing him to go free and to continue killing. And López did *plenty* of killing throughout the 1970s. On average, he raped and murdered three girls or young women per week at the height of his spree. López pretty much maintained the same MO: he'd find a girl in a market, entice her with promises of money and/or food, and then rape and murder the girl when he got her to an isolated area.

López was finally captured in 1980 when he attempted to abduct a girl from a crowded market in Ecuador. The girl's mother happened to be watching. She raised the alarm with others in the market, who quickly beat López and held him until the police arrived.

The police had a feeling that López was responsible for much more than an attempted abduction, so they used an informant to get López to confess to several murders. López eventually pled guilty to 57 murders but admitted to 110. He was given the maximum sentence in Ecuador at the time of 16 years. He was released early for good behavior after serving only 14 years!

López was then deported to his home country of Colombia where he faced murder charges. Most people thought that would be the end of the story, but instead, it all took another bizarre turn. The court ruled that he was insane and was to be held in a mental hospital. Okay, well at least he wasn't out in society, right? Well, he is now. López was granted a $50 bail in 1998, which he promptly paid and left the hospital.

López's whereabouts are currently unknown, but most experts are convinced that he has killed again and will continue to kill. If you're planning on taking a trip to the northern Andean region, or you currently live there, be on the lookout for the Monster of the Andes and don't let your children stray too far. There is a true monster on the loose.

The Ninth President

If you don't know who the ninth President of the United States of America is offhand, don't worry, you're not alone. William Henry Harrison (1773–1841) is at the bottom of nearly every list of greatest American presidents, not necessarily for anything bad he did but because he was president for only 31 days. Harrison's was the shortest tenure of any American president and among the shortest in modern history by a leader who was not usurped or assassinated. So, who was William Henry Harrison, and why/how did he die after only being president for one month?

William Henry Harrison was born just before the American Revolution to a prominent Virginia family. He was a good student as a kid but proved to have an aptitude for the military when he fought in the Northwest Indian War (1785–1795). The war and the military gave Harrison political connections that he would use effectively throughout his life and it also introduced him to the land that he would call home the rest of his life.

Harrison served as a representative for the Northwest Territory and would later be a congressman and senator for the state of Ohio. By the time Harrison got the Whig Party's presidential nomination in 1840, he had built quite an impressive resume. Aside from the Northwest Indian War, Harrison was also a veteran of the War of 1812 and had represented Ohio in Washington for decades. He faced a tough election against incumbent Martin Van Buren, who was not afraid to sling plenty of dirt at Harrison.

One of the points that Van Buren and his supporters focused on was Harrison's age. In his late 60s during the campaign, Harrison was quite old to be a politician at that time. Back then, most politicians retired from public office in their 50s or 60s, so Harrison was bucking the trend. Those who attacked Harrison for his age argued that the president needed to be younger and virile. An older president was more susceptible to diseases and illness, they argued. No one could've guessed how right they were!

Largely based on the poor state of the American economy at the time, Harrison won an electoral college landslide victory in November and immediately began planning his move to Washington. Harrison was inaugurated on March 4, 1841, which proved to be what killed him. A number of factors came together that day to create the perfect storm that ensured Harrison would be America's shortest-serving president.

It was cold and rainy in Washington that day, which alone wouldn't have been enough to kill Harrison, but he didn't do himself any favors. Harrison campaigned as a frontiersman, so during his inauguration, he wanted to keep that image by not wearing a hat or overcoat. He also rode a horse during the parade instead of in a carriage. His inaugural speech was very long, meaning he was standing in the rain for more than two hours. Finally, he partied into the early morning hours, attending three different inaugural balls.

It was all too much for the old man. He fell ill with pneumonia on March 26, but his fate was still not certain. His doctors, though, inadvertently ensured that he'd die. Although medical science of the mid-1800s had advanced quite a lot compared to even 100 years earlier, bizarre treatments were still quite common.

Most doctors believed that the majority of illnesses were blood-related, so treatments often involved bleeding patients, sometimes via leeches. Harrison's doctors tried several home remedies and then decided to bleed him. The treatment only served to weaken the sick man more, hastening his death in the process.

The case of William Henry Harrison's death is certainly strange and fascinating, but it was avoidable. If Harrison would've simply worn a coat, he probably would've served at least one term and more people today would know who the ninth president was.

An Ominous Album Cover

In 1977, American rock band Lynyrd Skynyrd was hitting their stride. They had just recorded their fifth studio album, *Street Survivors*, had already recorded a platinum-selling album, and regularly played to sold-out stadiums. The band found a popular formula with their unique southern rock style that was heavy on the guitar yet short on social commentary.

The members of Lynyrd Skynyrd knew that people had grown tired of the often pretentious and preachy music of the 1960s, so they were more than happy to provide Americans with basically harmless party music. Many bands tried to copy Lynyrd Skynyrd's style, but there was only one Lynyrd Skynyrd.

When lead singer Ronnie Van Zant went into the studio in July 1977, he knew that they had to create something great that would outdo their previous albums. After working on *Street Survivors* for about a month, the seven members of Lynyrd Skynyrd were happy with what they had. With songs like "What's Your Name," "That Smell," and "You Got That Right," Van Zant knew that the album was destined to be a hit. And he was right. Chances are, even if you aren't a Lynyrd Skynyrd fan, you're at least somewhat familiar with those songs. They're staples at many bars around America and they've been used on the soundtracks of countless films and television shows. But a big part of the reason for *Street Survivors'* success came from what happened next.

After recording the album, the seven Lynyrd Skynyrd members did a typical photoshoot at MCA studios. Van Zant and the other band members wanted to have an album cover that would draw plenty of attention and still be related in some way to the title. They went with a photo of the band standing in a street engulfed in flames. Steve Gaines and Ronnie Van Zant were engulfed in the most flames, but the flames were around every member. It was cool, hip, and catchy, so the band gave the thumbs up and it went to press. Then tragedy struck.

On October 20, 1977, just three days after *Street Survivors* was released, a small plane carrying Ronnie Van Zant and guitarist Steve Gaines crashed in a Mississippi swamp, killing Van Zant, Gaines and four others. When news got out about the crash, fans were immediately horrified to see that the album cover seemed to foretell the tragedy. MCA immediately changed the album cover to a picture of the band standing in front of a black background. Despite the tragedy and controversy over the album cover, or maybe partially because of it, *Street Survivors* quickly became a platinum-selling album.

Alpha Centauri

Remember earlier in this book when we talked about Robot from the television show *Lost in Space*? The basic plot of that show had a family trying to get to the Alpha Centauri system where they could start a new human civilization. Along the way, they met all kinds of aliens, but in the end, they never reached their destination. So, what is Alpha Centauri, and is there a possibility that life exists there?

At just over four light-years away, Alpha Centauri is the name of the closest solar system to our own. Alpha Centauri is fairly unique because it is a binary system, which means that it has two stars that orbit around each other. The system's primary stars—Alpha Centauri A and Alpha Centauri B—are close to the same size and luminosity as our sun. Alpha Centauri A is a little bigger and hotter, while Alpha Centauri B is a little smaller and cooler. There is also Alpha Centauri C, but it is a red dwarf and not visible to the naked eye.

Alpha Centauri was believed to be just one star for several centuries. The Greek scientist Ptolemy observed and recorded Alpha Centauri in the 2nd century CE, but astronomer Jean Richaud was the first person to note that it was a binary system in 1689. Once it was determined that Alpha Centauri was the closest system to our own and that its two primary stars were of a similar size to the Sun, people began to wonder if life existed in the system. Of course, there are several prerequisites necessary for life. You need to have a planet and that planet needs to be within the habitable zone of its star. The habitable zone must be able to support life by having liquid water, breathable air, and air pressure that can be sustained by living beings.

Scientists so far have only definitively identified one planet in the Alpha Centauri system—Proxima Centauri b. Although Proxima Centauri b orbits the red dwarf, it is within the habitable zone. Despite being located within that "sweet spot," scientists believe that it would be difficult to sustain life on Proxima Centauri b because of high solar winds and the possibility that the planet is tidally locked. But let's just say, for the sake of argument, that life could be sustained in the Alpha Centauri system. How long would it take to get there?

Based on current technology, it would take a craft potentially thousands of years to travel from Earth to Alpha Centauri. Scientists believe that using solar sail crafts would drastically reduce that number and plan to send the first probe out by 2069. Who knows, maybe there are people like us in Alpha Centauri.

A Real Zombie?

There's no denying that zombies are a big part of pop culture and have been for about ten years. The current zombie craze began with the hit American television show *The Walking Dead* and later spread to just about every country on the planet. You can now find zombie movies and TV shows in Japan, Russia, and Latin America, and the trend doesn't seem to be slowing down anytime soon.

The recent zombie craze approaches the issue from the perspective that the zombie outbreak was caused by some sort of virus or another disease, but the early zombie films looked at it from a more supernatural perspective. The 1932 film, *White Zombie*, starring horror legend Bela Lugosi, was the first true zombie film. In *White Zombie*, people were turned into the undead through magic and various concoctions. It is certainly a far cry from the zombie culture of today, but is it far from reality?

When Clairvius Narcisse showed up in his Haitian village in 1980, his friends and family were beyond surprised to see him; they were bewildered, perplexed, and a bit frightened. You see, Narcisse hadn't been seen in his home village in more than 18 years, so his arrival was a surprise. However, the real kicker was that the last time anyone saw Narcisse, he was dead!

Narcisse's story began on April 30, 1962, when he checked into a hospital with a severe fever. After doing all they could for him, local doctors, as well as two American doctors, pronounced Narcisse dead. His body was released to his family, and he was buried on May 2. Then the story gets weird.

Probably within a day or two, a Voodoo sorcerer dug up Narcisse's body, beat him, and then forced him to drink a substance that made him the sorcerer's slave. For two years, Narcisse worked as a mindless slave on the sorcerer's plantation. The sorcerer gave Narcisse the minimal amount of food and water to survive and he was also sure to give him some of the substance that brought his zombie back to life. Then the sorcerer died.

After the sorcerer died in 1964, Narcisse's mind started to clear from the drug-induced fog. He was a lost man, though, and not sure what or who he was. He wandered Haiti for 16 years before returning to his home village. Narcisse's sister recognized him and after some trepidation, the people of the village accepted him. Clairvius Narcisse died (for a second time) in his home village in 1994.

Narcisse related his account to newspapers and scholars, describing a truly terrifying ordeal. Narcisse said that he was conscious when he was declared dead and buried. He also said that the two years after he was dug up and forced to work on the plantation was a haze. Most of the people of Haiti believed that Narcisse did die and was a zombie, but scholars from around the world were skeptical.

In the 1980s, ethnobotanist Wade Davis first advanced the theory that Narcisse, and other reported zombies in Haiti, were the victims of a drug cocktail. Davis argued that a tetrodotoxin from a pufferfish and bufotoxin from a toad were mixed and administered to Narcisse to put him in a coma. He was then woken through another drug, datura. Datura can have both stimulant and hallucinogenic effects, which allowed the sorcerer to effectively control Narcisse. But not everyone was convinced of Wade's work.

Although there are plenty of chemical concoctions in the Voodoo religion, more in-depth studies by other scholars after Wade have shown that the toxins needed to turn a person into a zombie are absent from all recipes used in known rituals. Of course, those are just the *known* recipes. If you were a Voodoo priest whose sugar plantation required mindless slaves to work it, would you give away your potion's secret ingredients?

It's Called Rasslin'

Today, there are plenty of sports that unite the different cultures and countries of the world. Football (soccer in some countries) is the most popular sport in the world and followed religiously by hundreds of millions and even more every four years during the World Cup.

After football/soccer, you have cricket, basketball, hockey, and baseball as the most popular team sports. Tennis and golf also rank quite highly among sports enjoyed by spectators from around the world. But one sport enjoyed by people from all around the world is often derided and not even considered a real sport—professional wrestling.

Hopefully, I don't need to say that professional wrestling is choreographed, and the outcomes are fixed. Notice, though, I didn't say it is "fake" because that would imply that the performers aren't doing anything dangerous or strenuous. And that simply isn't the case. Professional wrestling as we know it, whether done in Europe, North America, or Asia, is a combination of theatrics and athletics, with origins in both.

Professional wrestling developed simultaneously in the United States and Europe as part of carnival acts and sideshows. Carnival strongmen were pitted against each other in matches that had predetermined outcomes, although the intent was to keep the appearance of being "real." Many of the early wrestlers had backgrounds in amateur wrestling, so the matches often appeared as such.

Professional wrestling spread throughout the world after World War II, being introduced in Asia with military personnel and throughout Latin America via the United States, where high-flying performers developed a style of their own known as Lucha libre. Performers such as Gorgeous George brought the sport to living rooms across the world, as advertisers and television stations began seeing dollar signs. Eventually, by the 1970s and '80s, professional wrestling couldn't be ignored. It was loved by working-class people all over the world.

But as much as the working class loved professional wrestling, many urbanites and upper-class people thumbed their nose at it as lower class, provincial and, in the United States, redneck. Those who hated professional wrestling began referring to it as "rasslin'" in their best mock Southern accent.

But wrestling fans didn't care and kept going to events and watching it on television. They seemed to relish in the hatred of their sport, and ironically began calling it "rasslin'" themselves. By the 1990s, professional wrestling was a multi-billion-dollar industry and had become part of global pop culture. Who alive today, especially over the age of 30, doesn't know who Hulk Hogan is?

There is little doubt that professional wrestling has made a major impact on the economies and pop cultures of many countries around the world. No matter how low brow you may feel it is, or how often it's decried as not a real sport, the reality is that, due to its strong international appeal, "rasslin'" will be around for quite some time.

Not So Fast!

Today, there are more than 190 independent countries in the world, which range in age from very old (Egypt and China) to very new (South Sudan). Some countries were born out of turmoil (United States), while others were gradually given their independence (Canada and Australia). Perhaps the most ironic thing about countries and the world we live in is that, the more we move toward a globally integrated world, the more countries keep popping up throughout the world.

Part of the reason for the ever-growing number of countries is partly because countries, as we know them, are a pretty modern concept. In the ancient and medieval worlds, people were part of kingdoms and didn't see national identity in the same way. It wasn't until the 1700s that people began seeing themselves as part of nations.

The modern idea of a nation-state is based on the notion that people with a shared language and cultural identity should share the same borders. The concept has led to some wars in the 19th and 20th centuries, but it has also led to some interesting, and occasionally humorous, declarations of independence.

Do you remember the Catalonian independence movement in 2017? If you don't, don't feel bad because it wasn't long-lived. In the fall of 2017, people in the Spanish autonomous community (basically what the Spanish call a province) of

Catalonia began protesting against the Spanish government and demanded independence. Catalonia has always considered themselves somewhat different than the rest of Spain and likes to point out that their primary language is Catalan, not Spanish.

Well, the Catalonian political leaders announced their independence from Spain in October 2017, calling themselves the Catalan Republic. It sure looked like they would be the world's newest country, but Spanish Prime Minister Mariano Rajoy said, "not so fast, Catalonia." When Catalonia's leader Charles Puigdemont was threatened with arrest, he fled the country and the independence movement collapsed. But as ephemeral as Catalonia's independence may have been in 2017, there are other notable cases in recent world history.

Carpatho-Ukraine was once the most powerful country in Eastern Europe. Do you remember when? Neither do I because it only existed from March 15 to March 16, 1939. Carpatho-Ukraine was in a tough neighborhood during a tough time in history. It was bordered by Hungary, Slovakia, Poland, and the USSR, all of which were harboring imperial ambitions at the time. For some reason, leaders in the forested region thought that, by declaring independence and appealing to Nazi Germany, they could stay free. Instead, the Germans let their Hungarian allies conquer the region, and Carpatho-Ukraine was never heard from again.

The Faroe Islands declared their independence from Denmark after World War II, but after only two days, the King of Denmark, Christian X, said "no dice" and brought the archipelago back into the Danish fold. Some other modern countries that had their freedom stifled before they even had a real chance to enjoy it was the country of Somaliland, which was a nation-state for five days in 1960, the ten-month Kingdom of Lithuania in 1918, and the Democratic Republic of Yemen, which survived for just over a month in 1994.

It's hard to say for sure where the next short-lived nation-state will be, but before too long, one is bound to take Carpatho-Ukraine's title, right?

There Are More of These Than Stars

For most people (me included), once the number of something gets beyond 1,000, it becomes increasingly difficult to conceptualize. Unless you've had one million dollars in cold hard cash in front of you, it's pretty difficult to visualize just how big that pile is. The same goes for just about anything, and as the number goes up, it gets progressively harder to determine.

So, have you ever looked into the night sky and tried to guess how many stars are in the Milky Way galaxy? Right offhand, most people would probably say a few thousand, or maybe a couple million. You would be way off, my friend. Thanks to awesome telescopes, some excellent computer software, and several sharp minds, NASA scientists have estimated that there are up to 400 billion stars in the Milky Way galaxy. Yes, that's billion with a "b."

Surely, then, nothing on our planet could eclipse those numbers other than rocks and possibly the combined amount of money being printed by central banks, right? Well, there is one thing on our planet that outnumbers the stars in the galaxy by quite a bit—trees!

Yes, you read that right: there are more trees on Earth than stars in the galaxy; there are about three trillion trees currently on planet Earth, or about 420 trees per every person. Scientists arrived at that number using some of the same technology used to count the stars and it reveals some pretty interesting things about the resiliency and future of the planet.

Humans are responsible for cutting down about 15 billion trees annually, which means that at that rate, it would take under 200 years to cut down every tree. That's good news, of course, but many scientists warn that we should all practice good conservation habits and plant new trees whenever possible.

The Beach Boys
Meet Charles Manson

The 1960s was a turbulent time in the United States. Protests against the Vietnam War were a regular occurrence, and by 1968, they often turned violent. The civil rights movement had also morphed into a hotbed of violent extremism by the late '60s with the likes of the Black Panthers. Then there was the hippy subculture. Young people across the country were "tuning in" to their favorite rock bands and then "dropping out" of society.

For older, conservative Americans, the 1960s was a period of chaos where everything was turned upside down, but for many young people at the time, it was a fun period in their lives when they enjoyed their last true taste of freedom. Any positive feelings the '60s engendered in anyone quickly evaporated when psychopath Charles Manson and his "Family" went on a rampage in the summer of 1969, leaving nine people dead in southern California. The brutality of the murders shook the nation, and as members of the Family were arrested, what was already a strange case jumped up several levels of bizarre.

The more investigators learned about the little 5'2" career criminal known as Charlie, and the hold he had over his following of mostly young women, the more perplexing the case became. They learned that Manson and his Family were preparing for an epic race war in an abandoned ghost town in southern California, but as strange as that all was, the more investigators uncovered, the stranger the case became. The police learned that before Manson and the Family relocated to the isolated ghost town, they were squatting at Dennis Wilson's Los Angeles mansion.

That's Dennis Wilson, the drummer—and co-founder—of the iconic American surfer rock band, The Beach Boys. So, how did Dennis Wilson get mixed up with such a motley band of murderers, and how did he not become one of their victims?

The strange connection between the rock star and the serial killer began when Wilson picked up two hippy girls who were thumbing their way through upscale Malibu in the spring of 1968. He saw the same two girls a couple of weeks later, picked them up again, and brought them to his home on Sunset Boulevard. The two women happened to be Family members Patricia Krenwinkel and Ella Jo Bailey. Wilson immediately thought he had a connection with the young women, as they shared some marijuana and talked about spirituality. Wilson told the girls about his Indian guru while the girls told him about "Charlie."

Wilson left the two women at his home while he worked at a recording studio. When he returned later that night, he was met by Charlie and several other family members. They had essentially moved in and started squatting at Wilson's home, although Wilson didn't seem to mind at first. It was a party atmosphere and Wilson was a young rock star. There were plenty of women and drugs available, but more importantly, Wilson liked and respected Charlie.

You see, Manson was a bit of a musician himself—or at least he thought of himself as one. Manson recorded some of his songs in Wilson's home studio and Wilson, in turn, covered some of Manson's songs. The two men were fast becoming friends and it was noted by many that they even shared a resemblance, especially when both men wore beards.

Dennis introduced Manson to the other Beach Boys and brought him into their recording studio. "This is Charlie," Wilson said, upon their introduction. "He is the wizard, man. He is a gas." The other Beach Boys weren't so sure about Charlie. They thought he was a bad influence on Dennis, especially when they found out that Dennis had spent over $100,000 on feeding, clothing, and giving cars to members of the Family. A large part of that money was also spent on medicine for a gonorrhea outbreak among the "free love" Family members.

But there was a bit more that the Beach Boys didn't find right about Manson. He just seemed slightly off, yet they couldn't seem to put their finger on it. Then Charlie showed his true colors. Manson learned that one of the songs he wrote was being used by the Beach Boys, but it sounded nothing like what he originally wrote. He brought his problem to the Beach Boys and their producers, made some threats, and even pulled out a knife.

The relationship between the Beach Boys and Charles Manson ended that day. Manson gathered his Family and move out to the ghost town known as the Spahn Ranch where they planned their murderous spree. But Charlie never forgot the music business. Some of the victims may have been related to Manson's attempts to enter the industry.

The Family struck first on August 9, 1969, when they murdered actress Sharon Tate and four others at 10050 Cielo Drive in Beverly Hills. The location was important because it

114

was the address where music producer Terry Melcher had lived when Manson was trying to break into the music scene. Melcher was likely the intended victim and one or more of the Beach Boys may also have been on Manson's hit list.

As much as Dennis Wilson wanted to forget his involvement with Charles Manson and the Family, it continued to follow him until the day he died in 1983. And it all started with a seemingly innocent, chance encounter. I guess it's true what they say: be careful who you pick up hitchhiking.

Mexico's Zone of Silence

We've met a couple of strange and scary places in this book. Places that are believed to be haunted, regularly visited by aliens, or both. Perhaps what adds to the allure and legends surrounding these and other similar places is the setting—they are either located in isolated places or are old, run-down mansions. There are hundreds, if not thousands, of these types of places located throughout the world. Each has legends and histories of its own, as well as plenty of supporters, and detractors, of said legends.

If you're ever in the middle of the northern Mexican state of Durango and you want an adventuresome trip to see one of the world's creepiest locales, stock up on some water, gas, and other supplies and make your way to the Mapimí Biosphere Reserve. Once there, you'll find a sign out in the middle of the desert marked, "la zona del silencio," which indicates you've found the location: Mexico's Zone of Silence.

Mexico's Zone of Silence is an eerie, approximately 31-mile area where radio communication routinely fails, and people have reportedly gone missing without a trace. It has been compared to the better-known Bermuda Triangle, and in a somewhat freaky coincidence, both are located between the 26th and 28th parallels. Although, many people say there's no such thing as coincidence!

The Zone of Silence started to become a household name to many Mexicans and people in the paranormal community after an American experimental rocket went off course from New Mexico and landed in the Durango desert in 1970. The Americans were very interested in finding the rocket because it contained two containers of the radioactive material cobalt 57. The rocket and the cobalt 57 were found after a few weeks of searching, which is when things started to get a bit strange. A large team of American scientists and military came to the crash site, built a road to the rocket, and stripped the topsoil in the area.

After the Americans left, numerous reports of strange activity in the zone became quite common. Strange lights, radio silence, and the sudden appearance and then vanishing of mysterious people were routinely reported. But unexplainable activity in the zone began long before the American rocket crash.

One of the earliest reports of strange activity came in the 1930s when Mexican pilot Francisco Sarabia reported radio failure while flying over the region. Sarabia's experience was followed up when Harry de la Peña visited the region in 1964. Harry was an engineer for Mexico's state oil company and was there to survey the area for a pipeline. Harry had a difficult time completing his task because his radios wouldn't work. Frustrated, he began referring to the area as the "zona del silencio" and the name stuck.

Due to all the reported abnormal activity, UFO hunters and paranormal investigators have been attracted to the Zone of Silence in recent years, often to the chagrin of locals. Explanations for the anomalies range from the results of radiation to aliens, to the opening to another dimension.

Although the secrets of the Zone of Silence will probably never be solved, some of the exasperated locals have given in and decided to market merchandise for the Zone. It may be just a matter of time before you see "Zona del Silencio," t-shirts. Hmmm ... that isn't a bad idea!

Color or Colour?

How languages evolve is complex and contingent upon many factors. Most spoken languages today have changed tremendously since they were first born, making them, in many cases, almost new languages. The modern English language is no different.

Descended from a Germanic language root, which was in turn descended from an Indo-European root, the English language has gone through many changes in the last 1,500 years. After transitioning from Anglo-Saxon to Old English in the Middle Ages, modern English was born about 500 years ago. But it was still a very different language than what is spoken today. If you've ever read Shakespeare, you know that's true.

When British colonists began spreading their language around the world in the 1600s and 1700s, it didn't take long for it to change yet again. The basic style, grammar, and syntax of the language remained the same, but subtleties in the English language began to become apparent in the years after the American Revolution.

Eventually, the differences led to scholars differentiating between British English and American English. You've no doubt witnessed some of those minor variations in things you've read, or maybe you've watched some BBC America "telly" show and wondered what they meant when they said they were "going to load some blokes in the lorry at half three to make a few quid!" So, how did this divergence take place and what does it include besides vocabulary and spelling?

The simplest answer to the first part of the question is that American and British English began diverging after the American Revolution, but the true answer is a little more complex than that. A conscious move away from British culture didn't take place in the United States until after the War of 1812. For decades after that war, there was a genuine anti-British attitude in the United States, which eventually made its way into the American lexicon.

In 1828, Noah Webster of the *Webster's Dictionary* fame introduced unique American English spelling. It was in this, and all subsequent editions, that he suggested Americans spell color instead of colour, center instead of centre, tire instead of tyre, and recognize instead of recognise, among hundreds of other words. Webster developed a definite pattern with his new American spelling: "u" was dropped from words when it accompanied an "o" (parlor instead of parlour), "re" endings were substituted in favor of "er," and "z" became a common way to pronounce "s" sounds.

In addition to spelling, a slightly different vocabulary has also developed in the two countries. In Britain, they're called "blokes" while in the U.S., they're simply "guys"; a "lorry" is what Americans call a large truck; and a "quid" is simply slang for a British pound, just like the American slang for a dollar is a "buck."

There are, of course, other terms that are confusing to British or Americans, depending on who is uttering the terms and what country you are in. The British call cookies "biscuits," while Americans call holidays "vacations." The British say they are going "to hospital," while Americans say they are going "to *the* hospital," always with the definite article.

Now, you may be wondering, is this true across the entire Anglosphere? Well, again, that answer is a bit complicated. Most other English-speaking countries follow British English conventions, but Canada is a bit of a tricky case. Canadians tend to follow British spelling, but as much as they hate to admit it, they are heavily influenced by their southern neighbors. Canadians tend to "go on vacation," eat "cookies," and drive "trucks," much like Americans. Hockey is also Canadians' favorite sport and they get a kick out of it when they hear Brits call it "ice hockey." Even Yanks call it hockey!

Just remember, if you're a Brit reading this and you plan to visit the States, they say they "sweep things under the rug" instead of the carpet. And if you're an American planning on taking a holiday in the UK, Ireland, or Australia, know not to let any of your "skeletons out of the cupboard," not the closet, and you'll be fine.

The Colonial Parkway Killer

The Colonial Parkway is a 23-mile road that connects the historic cities of Jamestown, Williamsburg, and Yorktown. If you enjoy history, architecture, or some nice scenery, you'll get plenty as you drive along the Colonial Parkway. But be careful if you ever make the drive at night. Don't stop along the many turn-off spots, and watch who you pull over to help. Even better, don't make the drive at all at night unless you want to be the ninth victim of the Colonial Parkway killer. He's still on the loose, perhaps waiting to strike again.

The Colonial Parkway killer first struck on October 10 or 11, 1986. On October 12, the bodies of Cathleen Thomas (27) and Rebecca Dowski (21) were discovered murdered in the back seat of Thomas' car at an overlook of the Parkway. It was truly a horrific scene and can only be described as "overkill." Both women had rope burns on their wrists and necks and showed signs of strangulation, but it was the slashes to their throats that killed them. Curiously, neither woman had been sexually assaulted, and their money wasn't taken.

The killer—or killers—struck again about a year later when they killed a 20-old man and his 14-year-old girlfriend along the road. The couple was shot to death, placed in their car, and then the car was parked near the James River. A third couple went missing on April 10, 1988. Their car was found at a scenic overlook on the Colonial Parkway, but no bodies have ever been found.

A final pair of murders attributed to the Colonial Parkway killer took place on September 5, 1989, in New Kent County, several miles west of the Colonial Parkway. In that case, 18-year-old Annamaria Phelps and her 21-year-old friend, Daniel Lauer, were driving to Virginia Beach to meet Lauer's brother and Phelps' boyfriend. The pair never made it to Virginia Beach.

Lauer's car was discovered on the west-bound rest stop of Interstate 64, which was mysterious since the couple was heading east into Virginia Beach. The couple's skeletal remains were discovered on October 19, not far from the rest stop. The authorities believe the killer—or killers—may be responsible for a few more missing persons cases in the area, but it is difficult to say for sure.

Theories about who did the murders, how many people were involved, and how many victims there are abound; unfortunately, the case doesn't appear to be any closer to being solved. Many believe that more than one killer was involved, possibly working as a team, or that some of the murders were unrelated. The next question is: how was the killer able to kill so many couples so effectively?

The answer to this question may be related to the first. The Colonial Parkway killer may have been a pair of killers, which would have made it easier for them to control two victims at a time. The killer may also have posed as a police officer, allowing him to gain the trust of his victims and then strike. Whatever the Colonial Parkway killer's MO, it appears that he suddenly stopped killing in 1989. Could it be that he was arrested or died?

Most people like to think that when they learn that a serial killer hasn't been heard of for a while. Serial killers don't follow any particular rulebook, however, and their drives and motivations are as varied as their methods. So, it's truly anyone's guess why we quit hearing about the Colonial Parkway killer. He could have moved his show to another location or maybe he drastically changed his MO and began burying all his victims. He did conceal the bodies of his fourth and fifth victims effectively, so maybe that was a rehearsal for his later activities.

Or it could be the Colonial Parkway killer just decided to take some time off. Maybe he's getting ready to come out of retirement.

Al-Hakim, Where'd You Go?

Throughout world history, several notable people have disappeared off the face of the Earth. Amelia Earhart's 1937 disappearance in the South Pacific is perhaps the most famous in the world, but other notable disappearances include American Indian leader Sequoyah in 1843 and the vanishing of the entire Roanoke colony in the late 1500s.

Among all the people who disappeared in world history, Al-Hakim bi-Amr Allah—usually just abbreviated as Al-Hakim—was the most powerful, and certainly at the top of his game when he vanished. Most believe that the often-cruel leader was assassinated by one or more of his enemies, while others think he chose to follow his spiritual ambitions and become a hermit. Others still think the supernatural or the divine may have been behind Al-Hakim's disappearance.

Al-Hakim was born Abu Ali Mansur in 985 CE in Egypt to the caliph of the Fatimid Empire, Al-Aziz bil-Lah. As the caliph of the empire, it was Al-Aziz's duty to uphold Shia Muslim principles and to advance the physical boundaries of the caliphate whenever possible. Al-Aziz fought wars against other Muslims, as well as the Christian Byzantine Empire.

Interestingly though, Abu Ali Mansur's mother was a Christian woman named as-Sayyidah. He is said to have inherited his blue eyes and fair complexion from his mother, but none of her tolerance or humility. Once Abu became ruler, he would have no time for such traits.

Abu became ruler when he was just 11. His father died while on a diplomatic/military trip to Syria, which meant that Abu was coronated as the next caliph. His name was immediately changed to Al-Hakim and he began to learn the precarious ways of life at court. The royal treasurer and eunuch (yes, that means he had been castrated!), Barjawan, ruled as regent while Al-Hakim learned the ropes of royal power and studied religion with some of the best-known religious scholars in the Islamic world.

The result of Al-Hakim's education proved to be very unique. He was seen as very holy by many close to him and, as such, was viewed as a prophet by a growing number of people. Al-Hakim often spent much of his time meditating in the desert and writing about religious theology. Some of those who respected his spirituality went on to start the Druze religion, which played an important role in the Middle East's history in medieval and modern times.

But when Al-Hakim wasn't meditating or praying, he was probably killing people. When Barjawan was murdered in 1,000 CE, Al-Hakim officially assumed the reins of power and immediately began to purge the empire of all his enemies, real or perceived. After killing most of his political enemies, Al-Hakim was then able to turn his attention toward those he despised: religious enemies.

Although the majority of the Egyptian people at the time were Sunni Muslims, Al-Hakim was a militant Shia Muslim, so he tried to force the people to accept Shia traditions. After pushing his Shia program for a few years, he then turned to persecuting the Christians and Jews. Egypt is home to one of the world's first organized Christian communities, which has had plenty of influence on Christian theology and has created beautiful church architecture.

Despite Egypt's Christian heritage, or maybe because of it, Al-Hakim banned Christians from celebrating Christmas and Easter and forced Christians to wear an iron cross in public. Al-Hakim also forced Jews to wear distinct clothing in public and members of both the Jewish and Christian communities were banned from using alcohol in their rituals. Then Al-Hakim followed all this up by destroying many of Egypt's churches and synagogues or by converting them into mosques. He even closed the Christian sites in Jerusalem and attempted to destroy the Holy Sepulcher. And to top all this off, he attempted to force all the non-Muslims in his empire to convert to Islam.

Although Al-Hakim later eased up on the Christians and Jews after 1012, the damage he had caused to those communities was extensive. Al-Hakim had created countless enemies throughout his empire at that point, but he didn't seem to care. He spent more and more time meditating in the desert and developing the theology of what would later become the Druze religion.

The evening of February 12, 1021 was just like many others for Al-Hakim. He loaded his donkey with supplies and headed out to the desert hills just outside of Cairo to meditate and commune with god in solitude. Al-Hakim never returned.

The caliph's loyal subjects searched for him, but only found his donkey and some bloody garments. Those who believed Al-Hakim was a prophet thought that he simply went away and will return someday to mark the beginning of the apocalypse. Others think that he ascended into heaven to sit at god's right hand. One of the more interesting modern theories is that Al-Hakim was abducted by aliens.

Still, the most probable explanation is something much more mundane. He may have simply wandered off, got disoriented, and then died from dehydration. The jackals and other scavengers would've quickly consumed his entire body, leaving only the bloody garments.

Or someone may have had him killed. Al-Hakim was not a very popular leader. He managed to anger just about everyone in Egypt by the time he was only 36, and many of those enemies were in his family. Some believe that his half-sister, Sitt al-Mulk, who was a practicing Christian, had him assassinated. Whatever happened to Al-Hakim, it'd be safe to say he wasn't missed.

The Color of Oxygen

Breathing is something that very few of us think about. It's just something that our body does unconsciously, and because of that, most of us probably don't think much about the air we breathe and the conditions that make the air breathable. It all comes down to oxygen!

Our atmosphere is about 78% nitrogen and about 21% oxygen, but it is the oxygen that keeps us alive. Once it gets below about 16%, humans will quickly die and if it gets too far above 20%, things can blow up pretty fast. The air we inhale is about 20% oxygen, but the air we exhale is only about 15% oxygen because the precious element is needed to regulate our circulation, which in turn regulates the rest of our bodies.

Since oxygen is so important to maintaining human life, have you ever thought about what it *looks* like? You're probably thinking that oxygen doesn't look like anything and also that it has no taste or smell. Well, you'd be partially correct. Oxygen in its *gas* form has no color, odor, or taste, but since elements can be transformed into all three states, oxygen does have a color.

Liquid oxygen is a light blue color, while solid oxygen can be colored red, black, or metallic. Although some people claim to be able to taste the oxygen in the air, scientists remain unconvinced and don't recommend trying to eat solid or liquid oxygen.

Football's Ironman

American football—or gridiron as it is sometimes called—is a tough sport. Those not familiar with the sport may think that the helmets and pads the players wear make the sport somewhat soft, but you only have to look at injury reports and long-term health problems, namely concussions and brain injuries, that players have sustained to see that it is physically demanding. So, professional players in the National Football League (NFL), Canadian Football League (CFL), and the indoor leagues generally have short careers.

It is considered pretty good if you can play professional football for five years, and if you can make it to ten years, then you should be set for life. But what about playing professional football for 27 years?

George Blanda was able to compete for 26 years in the NFL and American Football League (AFL) (the AFL was a separate league until 1970). By the time he retired in 1976, he was the first player to play in four different decades—only one of two today—and was also the oldest player to play a game at 48. And perhaps the most amazing part of George Blanda's career is that he played multiple positions. Although Blanda was a placekicker for most of his career, he was also a quarterback, which meant that he was routinely getting beaten up.

By the time he finally retired, Blanda had led the AFL in passing yards twice, passing touchdowns once, and even threw an amazing seven touchdowns in a game. Due to a combination of his longevity and on the field prowess, Blanda was elected to the NFL Hall of Fame in his first year of eligibility.

Blanda's long and illustrious career began in 1949 with the Chicago Bears, but head coach George Halas was never a believer in Blanda's versatility, so he primarily used him as a placekicker. Upset with being relegated to the second-string after an injury, Blanda retired from the Bears and professional football in 1958. Blanda decided to dedicate his time to his wife Betty and their two children, but by 1960, the love of the game was pulling Blanda back to the gridiron.

But what NFL team would take a gamble on a 33-year-old retired, second-string quarterback? The answer at the time was none, so Blanda decided to take his talents to the upstart American Football League. The AFL had its inaugural season in 1960 with eight teams, including the Houston Oilers. The Oilers were owned by a brash Texas oilman named Bud Adams, whose goal was to make Houston into a "major league" city that rivaled Dallas. Many people thought that he was also crazy when he signed "old man" George Blanda to a free-agent contract, but the gamble quickly paid off. Blanda led the Oilers to two AFL championships and set many records in the process.

Blanda played with the Oakland Raiders from 1967 until his retirement in 1976, mainly as a placekicker and backup quarterback, but he did have a few notable games. In a 1970 game, he came off the bench when first-string quarterback Daryle Lamonica was injured for several games.

In a November 8 game against the Cleveland Browns, Blanda proved to the world that he still had it. In the game, Blanda threw a touchdown pass with less than a minute remaining, to tie the game. Then, after the Raiders' defense held and got the ball back, he marched his team down the field and kicked the game-winning field goal with three seconds left!

George Blanda may not have been the flashiest player in professional football history, and he threw a lot of interceptions, but he was certainly one of the toughest. Based on the way the game is played today, it seems improbable that his longevity records will ever be surpassed, not only making him the true ironman of professional football but among the true ironmen in all professional sports history.

A Living Dinosaur?

You've probably seen one of the many movies in the *Jurassic Park* franchise, where well-meaning but misguided entrepreneurs and scientists combine their efforts to bring back species that have been extinct for more than 65 million years. Of course, the experiments go wrong—again and again and again—when the prehistoric creatures cause havoc and destruction on the world. As violent as the films are, they are also a bit humorous. I mean, this could never happen. Or could it?

The idea of bringing dinosaurs back to life through a variety of scientific methodologies is currently far outside human capacity, so you don't have to worry about your city being overrun by a hungry tyrannosaurus rex, but some people entertain the possibility that Jurassic Era creatures may still be living on Earth.

You've probably heard of the Loch Ness Monster, right? Many people think that it is a remnant plesiosaur that somehow escaped the K-T extinction—which was either the result of a large meteor, a series of super volcanoes, or both—that killed all the dinosaurs. Then this plesiosaur somehow survived several subsequent ice ages.

But the Loch Ness Monster is not the only dinosaur some believe escaped the K-T event. There have been numerous reports by locals and foreigners in central Africa of a creature that resembles a brontosaurus. Native Africans call this creature Mokele-mbembe, which in the Lingala language means "one who stops the flow of rivers," with many swearing that it is a legitimate animal. Other locals believe that Mokele-mbembe is a spirit creature, more like a ghost or demon, while most scientists believe that sightings are a combination of active imaginations, the dense jungles, and the lure of native folklore.

The Congo River Basin covers nearly four million square miles, primarily in the nation of the Democratic Republic of Congo, but parts lie in neighboring countries. The Congo River Basin is known for its dense forests, rivers and lakes, and diversity of peoples: this is the traditional home of the Aka (Pygmy) people.

The Congo River Basin has long been the source of many African folk tales, but reports of dinosaurs didn't become common until German explorers and big game hunters began visiting the area in the early 1900s. German big game hunter Carl Hagenbeck first reported brontosaurus-type creatures running around Africa in his autobiography *Beasts and Men*, although his claims were generally disregarded as unscientific and publicity-seeking.

In 1911, another German explorer named Paul Gratz claimed to have gone hunting for Mokele-mbembe on Lake Bangweulu but was ultimately unsuccessful, although he did claim to have found some of its skin. Other reported sightings of Mokele-mbembe were made by Westerners throughout the 20th century, yet few have been able to capture photos of the elusive creature. Believers say that a 1987 video of a large creature swimming across a lake in the Congo River Basin is proof of Mokele-mbembe but the image on the video could be anything. Photos that are supposedly of the creature's footprints have also surfaced from time to time (a la Big Foot), but of course, those are easy to fake.

Anthropologists claim that the stories are simply based on local legends, and reported sightings are of crocodiles, hippopotami, and other animals of the rainforest. Other scientists say that the stories of Mokele-mbembe sightings are just promoted by creationists who believe the Earth is much younger than scientists state and that dinosaurs and humans did live together, just as they did on *The Flintstones*.

But there is a group of believers who claim that the Mokele-mbembe is simply what is left of a species that survived the K-T extinction. It's hard to believe that a breeding population of an animal that is larger than an elephant could survive without being captured by humans, but if there is anywhere on this planet where it could escape detection, it would be in the Congo River Basin.

Too Many Similarities

Do you believe that coincidences are just the result of random chance and merely a series of events lining up at the right place at the right time? Or do you believe that there is no such thing as coincidence and that everything happens for a reason? Well, after reading this next story, you'll be able to tell which camp you fall into.

You no doubt know about Abraham Lincoln, the 16th president of the United States of America, and John F. Kennedy, the 35th president. You also probably know that both men were assassinated while in office, which puts them into the macabre fraternity of the four assassinated American presidents. But then the similarities start piling up.

Both men had seven letters in their last names and both presidents were first elected in '60—Lincoln in 1860 and Kennedy in 1960. Lincoln's 11-year-old son William died in the White House, while Kennedy also lost a son who died in the White House.

Lincoln's presidency was engulfed by the Civil War, while Kennedy's was during the height of the Cold War: the Cuban Missile Crisis almost led to World War III in 1962. Racial politics also played a major role in each man's presidency: for Lincoln, it was slavery and for Kennedy, it was the civil rights movement.

Both men were shot in the head on a Friday in the presence of their wives. Lincoln was shot in a theater by John Wilkes Booth, who fled to a warehouse. Lee Harvey Oswald shot Kennedy from a warehouse and fled to a theater. Both assassins, who are known by their infamous three names, were from the South and never lived to see trial. The full names of each assassin contain 15 letters. Lincoln's successor was Andrew Johnson, while Kennedy's was Lyndon Johnson. Both successors were from Southern states and were born in '08 (1808 and 1908).

Although the list of similarities may seem staggering and potentially point to something larger at work in the cosmos, skeptics point out that numerous similarities can be drawn between any two people and that many world leaders have more similarities due to their roles. With that said, it all comes back to the fact that Lincoln and Kennedy are among only four American presidents to have been assassinated. If you start with that single fact and work from there, then the similarities do seem uncanny. And a bit creepy.

Lollapalooza

If you're of a certain age, you probably remember the Lollapalooza music tour of the 1990s. If you don't, it was a multi-state, multi-city tour that featured some of the top names in rock and alternative music of the era, so there was plenty of hair, flannel, and beer to go around. Chances are you never thought much of the name of the tour, other than possibly thinking it was just some strange-sounding word that some grunge aficionado thought was cool.

Well, there's a lot more to the word lollapalooza than a music tour. Lollapalooza is a word that indicates something is outstanding or impressive, but it became an important word because it is what is known as a shibboleth. Shibboleth is an ancient Hebrew word that relates to how a particular word or words are pronounced by one group of people that separates them from other people.

In the original example, the word shibboleth, which refers to a part of a grain plant, was used by the people of Gilead to identify their enemies from Ephraim. The Ephraimites were unable to pronounce shibboleth the same way as the Gileadites, which made identifying them easy. There have been many similar examples of shibboleths used in wars and persecutions throughout history, with the word "lollapalooza" being used by the Americans in World War II.

In the heavy and intense fighting in the Pacific Theater of World War II, the Japanese used many different tactics to infiltrate American Marine camps. Sometimes Japanese soldiers with a modicum of English knowledge would attempt to pose as an allied soldier (Filipino), or Asian-American Marine, to get into the American camp to either spy or commit acts of sabotage. Once the Americans learned that the Japanese were doing this, they came up with a shibboleth to prevent further incidents—make anyone of Asian appearance approaching a checkpoint say "lollapalooza."

You see, to native Japanese speakers, and many northeast Asians in general, there is a tendency to pronounce "Ls" as "Rs." So, when a Japanese spy with only minimal English knowledge attempted to repeat the word, it would sound like "Rorraparooza." The spy/saboteur would then be gunned down before making it inside the camp.

Shibboleths are deeply connected with accents, regional dialects, and vernaculars, but the important thing is that they are usually just a single word or a couple of words. Furtive shibboleths are shibboleths that are based on the choice of words a group uses more so than the pronunciation, although they can also be influenced by accents.

Since the United States is such a large and diverse country, shibboleths that give people's regional origins away abound. For instance, you can tell who a native Minnesotan is because they call casserole "hotdish" and parking garages "parking ramps." Besides their noticeable accents, people from the southeastern states give themselves away by calling cement "see-ment" and freeways "expressways."

Likewise, Illinoisans call highways that you drive on "tollways," while in the northeastern states, they are "turnpikes." On the other hand, Californians never say "interstate" before the name of an interstate highway, instead referring to it simply by the number. Californians are further differentiated by a shibboleth between north and south in their references to highways: in southern California, they add the definite article before the name of the highway, "the 5."

Texans call the Dallas metropolitan area "DFW," Minnesotans call Minneapolis-St. Paul the "Twin Cities," and San Franciscans never, ever call their city "Frisco." Most Americans call carbonated sugar drinks "soda," while in parts of the Midwest, it's "soda pop" or just "pop," but in the southeast, it is "Coke." No matter the brand or flavor, it's always Coke. And if you ever end up in Norfolk, Nebraska be sure to pronounce it "Nor-fork" so you can fit in with the locals.

The Great Brinks Heist

Boston, Massachusetts is a city with two definite personalities. The public face of Boston is that of one of America's oldest cities where the American Revolution took root. Millions of tourists come to Boston every year from all over the world to see the Old North Church and follow the path that Paul Revere took when he warned the city that the "British are coming!" Visitors also go to see Bunker Hill and dozens of museums and other world-class cultural attractions in the city.

Boston is also known for its top tier colleges and universities— Harvard, Boston College, and Boston University, just to name three—and its accompanying nightlife and generally progressive attitude. But if you go a little beyond the historical monuments, college bars, and coffee shops, you'll find a darker, seedier Boston.

Boston has long been the territory of powerful underworld figures. Italian immigrants on the north end of Boston developed rackets, but it was the Irish Mob that ruled the rest of the city. The Mafia may have been the big boys in New York, Philadelphia, and Chicago, but the Irish ran the labor unions and rackets in Boston.

In 1950, a couple of Irish-American gangsters in Boston named Joe McGinnis and Joe O'Keefe recruited a motley crew of career criminals to rob the Brinks building in Boston for

$2.775 million, making it the largest robbery in history at the time; it would remain so until 1984. The robbers remained on the run for several years, which led to the robbery becoming known as the crime of the century.

The crew planned their heist out long in advance by breaking into the building several times and making keys so that, when the time was right, they could enter and leave quickly. Just before 7:00 p.m. on January 17, 1950, McGinnis, O'Keefe, and nine other men entered the building wearing masks, tied up the guards, and made off with the loot. Easy peasy, right?

Well, pulling off a heist like that is one thing, but getting away with it is another thing altogether. There were just too many people involved in the heist and it didn't help that they were all cutthroat criminals. When O'Keefe and another gang member were arrested in Pennsylvania for a burglary, the situation began to quickly unravel.

O'Keefe claimed he didn't get his part of the heist, so he kidnapped another gang member. After the gang paid O'Keefe a ransom, they also put a contract on his life. Realizing that he had few options, O'Keefe decided to cooperate with the FBI in 1956. All the gang members were arrested and served time for the Brinks heist. They were released by 1971; at least, those who didn't die in prison.

But that was just the end of one chapter of this incredible crime story. Out of all that money that the gang members took from the Brinks building, only $57,000 was recovered. Where was the rest?

Legends began circulating almost as soon as the gang had been busted. There were rumors that the money was cached in various locations around Boston and other stories that the robbers had invested in legitimate businesses. Some even believed that the thugs invested their money in offshore accounts.

The FBI may have got their men when they put the gang behind bars for the Brinks heist, but then it became the IRS's turn to start digging around South Boston. The reality is that the robbers probably spent the loot over the decades on numerous things. Gang member Vincent Costa is thought to have bought some rural property with his $100,000 share of the heist, but later claimed he was cheated out of most of it by his son.

The authorities believe that the gang members spent most of the rest of the money on living expenses and invested much of it in poorly run business schemes. Other members spent their shares on their favorite vices: booze, drugs, and sex workers.

Beside O'Keefe, the other Brinks heist robbers kept their mouths shut until the days they died. Because most of the robbers followed the code of silence and due to their daring, well-planned heist, the Brinks robbers are still viewed as heroes by many in the criminal underworld.

The Incredible
Shrinking Planet

As humans look into the stars for our future and the potential for life off the planet somewhere, most attention is on Mars, the asteroid belt, and beyond. Mercury and Venus are often overlooked, but due to the work of astronomers and other scientists, there has been a renewed interest in the two innermost planets. Most scientists will tell you that much can be learned about the Earth's very distant future by examining Mercury and Venus. If we are to learn anything from that, it's that our planet will someday be a lot smaller. At least that is what's been happening to the first planet, Mercury.

Mercury is a small planet, not much bigger than the Moon, which is tidally locked to the Sun, leading to some pretty extreme temperatures. It also has no atmosphere, creating surface temperatures that can get below -280 °F at night to 800 °F in the day. But the most amazing part about Mercury's physical composition is that it's shrinking. Yes, you read that correctly, Mercury is getting smaller.

For quite some time, scientists believed that Mercury was shrinking since its core is solid. At one time, the core of Mercury was heated, but once it turned into a solid piece of iron, it cooled, and the planet began to slowly shrink. This was all a theory until NASA launched the MESSENGER probe in 2004. The probe flew over Mercury 4,000 times, sending back thousands of images to Earth before it crashed in 2015.

After looking at the images, scientists were delighted to find that there were several scarps across Mercury, indicating that it is not only shrinking but that it is also tectonically active. Although Mercury may be at the end of its very long life cycle, it's still very active and appears to be going out with a bang. The shrinking Mercury may be what is in store for Earth billions of years in the future; that is if we don't do something to end it all before then.

The Most Popular Game
in the Wild West

When you watch television shows or movies set in the late 1800s American frontier, there is sure to be a scene when the characters are gambling in a casino or bar. Usually, they are playing poker, or sometimes it's blackjack. But in the most historically accurate movies, they're playing faro.

Faro was the most popular card gambling game in America in the late 1800s, much more popular than poker. Lawmen, madams, outlaws, and cowboys all played faro in the Wild West. Anyone trying to establish themselves in the Wild West had to know their way around a faro table. So, what was faro and why did it become so popular?

Faro is a card game that originated in France in the 1600s but was banned there and made its way to England and the German-speaking kingdoms. Immigrants brought faro to the United States in the early 1800s and by the late 1800s, it was the number one game in the country. The lure of making a quick buck and its easy-to-learn gameplay made faro very popular.

Like poker, blackjack, and other popular card gambling games, faro is played with a "shoe" of cards that consists of a 52-card deck and an additional 13 cards of each rank but single suits.

A faro dealer, known as a banker, would place the additional 13 cards of each rank, usually spades, face up on the table. These cards are called the board. The game then begins when the dealer burns the first card in the deck and then turns over two cards from the deck at a time. The first card is the losing card and the second card is the winning card. Bets are won and lost on the number, not suit, of the bets placed and the cards flipped.

So, if a player put their chip—or chips—on the two of spades and the two of hearts was the first card, then that player loses. Likewise, if the two of hearts was the second card then the player wins. Flipped cards are then burned, making counting easier. If both cards flipped are the same number and someone bet on it, then that player only loses half.

There are also many side bets in a faro game. A player can also bet that a winning card will be higher than a losing card by "betting the high card." A player can also insure their bet by placing a penny on it, betting that it will be the losing card.

Burned cards are kept face up for the players to see and count, which decreases the odds for the house. A dead bet is when a player places a bet on a rank that has been burned. Another player or dealer can take the bet if they notice. A player could also make a side bet on the order of the last three cards in the shoe.

Faro was largely replaced by poker and blackjack as the most common card gambling games in America in the early 1900s and the last Las Vegas casinos got rid of their faro tables in 1985. But faro didn't die out due to a lack of popularity; it was quite the opposite. Faro died out because it was terrible odds for the house. Players only had to have basic card-counting skills to help themselves.

147

Due to modern casinos being managed by corporations that examine every detail to try to widen their often thin profit margins, it's doubtful you'll see faro at your favorite casino anytime soon. However, now that you know the rules, nothing is stopping you and your buddies from playing faro instead of poker next weekend. After all, if it was good enough for Marshal Dillon, it should be good enough for you.

The Dragon and the Crow

When actor, stuntman, and martial arts expert Bruce Lee died on July 20, 1973, it was a case of a life gone too soon. He was only 32 and had a long career in front of him. Everything was going great for Lee in the early 1970s: he had fame, money, and success. He also had a young son, Brandon, a wife, and properties on two continents. He had just kicked Chuck Norris' butt (yes, *the* Chuck Norris) in the 1972 film *Way of the Dragon* and his mainstream crossover flick *Enter the Dragon* was set to come out in a couple of months. It all seemed so appropriate since Bruce Lee was born in 1940, the year of the dragon.

The exact cause of Lee's death made it seem a little mysterious, which ultimately started talk of a "Bruce Lee curse." After filming *Enter the Dragon*, Lee began having seizures and severe headaches and was diagnosed with a cerebral edema or fluid on the brain. It came as a shock to Lee, who prided himself on clean living and physical fitness, but prescription drugs reduced the swelling and he seemed to be on the road to recovery.

What happened next to Bruce is a source of controversy and may never be known for sure. While spending time with friends and business associates in Hong Kong on July 20, he began having headaches, so his friend Betty Ting give him a pill that contained aspirin and a tranquilizer. Within hours,

Lee was dead from a swollen brain, which doctors attributed at least partially to the pill, calling it "death by misadventure."

Others think Lee's death was caused by the overuse of cortisone, while some believe that it was the result of heatstroke from working too much. But some think that Lee, and later his son Brandon, never had a chance. They believe that Lee and his son were the victims of an ancient Chinese curse.

There are generally three versions of the Lee family curse. The first is that Bruce's father upset some influential people in Hong Kong who then brought down a generational curse on the family. Another is that, after he died, Bruce's father was buried next to a child, which is a no-no in Chinese culture.

The third and most interesting of the theories is that the curse originated in San Francisco's Chinatown. According to this version, after Lee moved to the United States in 1959, he began teaching his martial arts secrets to Americans, angering the older, more conservative Chinese of Chinatown in the process. The elders supposedly arranged a street fight between Lee and a man they chose, with the deal being that, if Lee lost, he had to quit teaching non-Chinese their secrets. If he won, he could keep teaching, unbothered by any of the elders. Lee won the fight, but as the theory goes, some of the elders decided to renege on their agreement by cursing Bruce and his entire family.

There wasn't much talk about the curse until Bruce's son Brandon died in a bizarre prop accident during the filming of the movie *The Crow* on March 31, 1993. The accident took place when a scene was being shot in which Lee's character was shot and killed. The gun used in the scene was a very real

.44 Magnum, but the bullets were blanks, which should've harmlessly emitted some powder and loud noise.

Unknown to Brandon, the prop crew had used "dummy rounds" in the gun in a previous scene. The crew made dummy rounds of their own by taking the bullets from the rounds, emptying the powder, and then replacing the bullets. The point was to give the effect that they were real rounds when the gun was shown being loaded, without it ever being fired.

But the gun was fired at some point and there just happened to be enough primer in the round to send it partially into the barrel where it'd only be seen upon careful inspection. The gun wasn't carefully inspected before Brandon's death scene. When the gun was fired, there was enough energy from the blank to project the stuck bullet from the gun at about the same velocity as it would normally, striking Brandon in the stomach. He died six hours later in the hospital at the age of 28.

The circumstances surrounding Brandon Lee's death were all a bit strange and creepy. The tragic series of mistakes was so bizarre and something that is, for the most part, unheard of on movie sets. Then there was the background of the movie and the character he was playing. In case you aren't familiar with *The Crow*, it is about a man (played by Brandon Lee) who is murdered as his girlfriend is beaten and raped. He then comes back from the dead to exact revenge on the perpetrators.

When news about the "curse" began circulating, it all just seemed very surreal. For many, it seemed that the supernatural was the only explanation for it all. If the Lee family was cursed, though, it all ended with Brandon, because he had no children.

That Scared the Hiccups Right Out of Me!

We've all had the hiccups at some point in our lives, and for some of us, they can be a very common, and annoying, occurrence. They often hit in the most embarrassing of moments. Maybe you're having a drink at a bar, talking to—or attempting to talk to—a nice-looking romantic interest, when all of a sudden … hiccups!

Or maybe you have to give an important presentation at work and you're feeling a bit nervous. Right before it's your time to shine, you start hiccupping like a frog. Or when you're about to meet your partner's parents for dinner and you just start hiccupping.

Yes, hiccups usually happen at inopportune moments because they can be caused by a variety of different factors. Hiccups originate in the muscle located between the lungs and the stomach known as the diaphragm. The diaphragm plays an important role in breathing, so when it's upset in any way, it causes spasms that result in a person sucking air into their throat.

The sucking leads to the sound known as hiccups. Most hiccups are caused by irregular swallowing, stress, and anxiety, or carbonated beverages such as beer, but more serious trauma to the diaphragm can cause long-term hiccups that can last weeks, months, or even years. But for the vast majority of hiccups cases, they can be easily and quickly cured.

There are many home hiccup remedies that people will swear are effective. Standing on your head while you drink water is one that is a bit complex yet useful. Another interesting one is to suddenly frighten the person afflicted with the hiccups. Now, I can personally attest to having tried both of those methods and having them work, or at least I thought they worked. But experts point out that there is no scientific data to back up either and that any success can be chalked up to a placebo effect.

So, what should you do then if you need to quickly get rid of the hiccups? The most effective and scientifically-sound ways to cure the hiccups seem to be simply holding your breath for as long as possible or breathing into a paper bag. Scientists point out that both methods cause a carbon dioxide buildup in your lungs, which can relax the diaphragm.

So, the next time you're at the bar chatting someone up and you feel a frog coming out of your throat, don't worry. Just take a deep breath—and if that doesn't work take another, and another. If that doesn't get rid of your hiccups, your potential date will probably get up and leave, so it won't matter anyway.

Ensuring Her Virtue

The Renaissance (1400s–1500s CE) was truly a different time in history. As the name indicates, there was a rebirth of art that was influenced by the ancient Greeks and Romans, new scientific theories were being tested, and humans began to see themselves as more important and not just as slaves before god. Many today see it as a truly enlightened time compared to the previous Middle Ages, but this wasn't always the case.

Punishment for criminals and/or criminal offenses was still quite swift and was often cruel (remember the guillotine story?) and ideas about sex, marriage, and equality were far from what they are today. As one stark example of this, we have the chastity belt. Chastity belts were literally what they said they were: metal belts that served to protect a woman's chastity.

The few known examples that exist, such as one that belonged to Catherine de' Medici (1519–1589), of the famous and powerful Medici family of Florence, now in the Musée de Cluny in Paris, are a bit scary to even look at, never mind consider wearing one. They resembled metal underwear with a lock that the key was presumably held by the wearer's husband or father. There were openings so the wearer could defecate and urinate.

You're probably now wondering, as I initially was: if there are openings in the belt in those two areas, what does it stop?

Well, the answer to that is where this all gets a bit scary, and possibly gruesome. Some of the extant examples have jagged "teeth" so that, if the wearer's chastity was challenged in any way, the violator would—well, let's just say, "have a mess" during any attempted sex!

Yes, the concept of the chastity belt is somewhat extraordinary, so much so that some historians claim that they were quite rare and are, in large part, more of a modern idea. The earliest definite mention of a chastity belt was in a 1405 book written by the German Konrad Kyeser, who many believe applied the term humorously, as a metaphor more than anything. Some historians also believe that the Renaissance chastity belts so prominently displayed in museums are from the 1800s.

Even if the chastity belts on display in museums do come from the 1800s, it doesn't take away from the fact that someone had to think of that. I like to think I have a pretty active imagination, but I never would come up with something like that—would you?

Maybe He Wanted to Get Caught

You've probably heard it said that certain serial killers wanted to be caught, or sometimes the killers themselves have said as much. Jeffrey Dahmer related that he felt relieved after being arrested and that a part of him wanted to get caught when he was at the height of his murderous rampage.

Although we can never know for sure what's in a person's heart and mind, it seems hard to believe that any serial killer ever wanted to get caught. Sure, some like Dahmer got pretty brazen and almost open with their activities, but it's just as easy to believe that their actions had more to do with arrogance than any sort of remorse.

No, serial killers murder as long as they can, with no remorse. Some may stop killing, but they don't want to get caught because they just don't see the world—and other people—the way most of us see it. This seems to be the case with pretty much every known serial killer, with the possible exception of one man: Paul Michael Stephani, the "Weepy-Voiced Killer."

Stephani was a rather unimpressive man throughout an otherwise unimpressive life. He was born in the southern Minnesota town of Austin in 1944 but later moved to St. Paul for better opportunities. But nothing seemed to go right for Stephani. He was divorced, couldn't get a girlfriend, and he couldn't hold down a job. In reality, he had more of the profile of a mass murderer than a serial killer, but the latter is how he became infamous. Well, sort of.

Stephani was also pretty unimpressive as far as serial killers go. He killed three women in 1981 and 1982, which barely makes him a serial killer, and he was beaten bloody by one of his intended victims. No, what makes Stephani interesting as far as serial killers are concerned is that it does appear that he wanted to get caught. He made numerous calls to the local police in a weepy voice asking, "Why haven't you stopped me?" until finally he was caught. Truly, when it comes to serial killers, Paul Stephani may not have had a high kill count, and he certainly wasn't one of the more depraved serial killers, but there is no doubt that the Weepy-Voiced Killer was one of the weirdest serial killer cases in American history.

Paul Stephani's reign of terror began on New Year's Eve 1980, in St. Paul, Minnesota. Stephani had just lost another factory job and he was lurking around the building, contemplating some revenge when a 20-year-old University of Wisconsin, Stevens Point student, Karen Potack walked by him.

Stephani later said that something just snapped. The below zero temperature meant that few people were out walking on the street, so Stephani was able to beat Potack and leave her for dead before fleeing the scene. He then called 911, directing the police to the location of the attack saying, half crying, "There is a girl hurt there."

Although Potack lived, Stephani would have another try at murder. He met 18-year-old Kimberly Compton at the iconic Mickey's Diner in downtown St. Paul on June 3, 1981. Like Potack, Compton was a student in Wisconsin, and also like Potack, she suffered Stephani's sick wrath. He stabbed and strangled Compton, leaving her lifeless body in a vacant lot.

Then Stephani made another call. "God damn, will you find me? I just stabbed somebody with an ice pick. I can't stop myself. I keep killing somebody." Stephani then called 911 two days later and said, "I'll try not to kill anyone else," and that he "couldn't help it. I don't know why I stabbed her. I'm so upset about it." The St. Paul Police began referring to the mysterious attacker as the "Weepy-Voiced Killer" and the moniker was eventually picked up by the local media.

Stephani waited more than a year to claim his next victim, but he changed his MO, so it went unnoticed for several years. On July 21, 1982, Stephani paid a visit to a female acquaintance named Kathleen Greening in the St. Paul suburb of Roseville. He drowned Greening in her bathtub and left the scene undetected. He also never called 911 to report the murder.

Stephani struck again a couple of weeks later in the neighboring city of Minneapolis on August 5. After spending the night drinking at a bar, he met a 40-year-old nurse named Barbara Simons who took an interest in the rather average-looking Stephani. The Weepy-Voiced Killer took Simons to an isolated location near the Mississippi River and stabbed her to death.

He then made a final call to 911. "Please don't talk, just listen … I'm sorry I killed that girl. I stabbed her 40 times. Kimberly Compton was the first one over in St. Paul." Stephani was finally caught when he attempted to stab a sex worker to death with a screwdriver, but she fought back by breaking a bottle across his face. He later called for medical help from his apartment and thanks to press coverage of the case, the operator recognized the voice on the line as the Weepy-Voiced Killer. Stephani was convicted of Simons' murder and sentenced to life in prison.

In 1997, Stephani learned he had terminal cancer, so he decided to come clean and confess to the murders of Compton and Greening. Although he was the only suspect in Compton's murder, he wasn't even on the police radar in the Greening case. "I'd rather go to the grave knowing this is all taken care of and off my chest," Stephani said about confessing to the two murders.

He died about a year after making the confessions, leading some to believe that he truly felt remorse. Maybe he did want to get caught, or maybe Paul Stephani was just a really weird guy.

That Dirty Little Coward
That Shot Mr. Howard

Jesse James is arguably the greatest American anti-hero. After serving in pro-Confederate guerilla bands during the Civil War, Jesse and his brother Frank formed a gang and became two of the most innovative criminals in American history. The brothers, and the gang they formed with the Younger brothers, performed some of the first daylight bank robberies in American history and were among the earliest train robbers.

As Jesse and his gang robbed trains and banks across the Midwest in the 1870s, his reputation grew into legendary status. He was viewed by former Confederates like himself as a freedom fighter and others secretly cheered him as he "stuck it" to the banks. But the life of a criminal is tough and when things get tough, they get tough.

When Jesse and his boys had a bank robbery foiled in Northfield, Minnesota on September 7, 1876, the gang was devastated, with most being either killed or captured. Jesse was able to escape, eventually ending back in his hometown of St. Joseph, Missouri under the alias Thomas Howard. He then attempted to start a new gang with brothers Charley and Robert Ford, but that was a big mistake. The Ford brothers only joined to collect the $5,000 reward on Jesse's head, so on April 3, 1882, Robert decided to collect.

He shot Jesse in the back of the head as he straightened a picture on the wall. The act was commemorated in a popular folk song that has been recorded by such wide-ranging pop artists as the Kingston Trio and Bruce Springsteen. Maybe you've heard it?

"Jesse James was a man that was knowed through all the land
For Jesse he was bold and bad and brave
But that dirty little coward that shot down Mr. Howard
Has went and laid poor Jesse in his grave"

Jesse's body was identified by his family members, which was confirmed by officials who observed two gunshot wounds and a missing middle finger on the body. Photographs were taken of Jesse James in a coffin and—other than a somewhat lengthy beard—it looked like him. Or did it?

Almost as soon as Jesse James was laid to rest, conspiracy theories began circulating in America that he was still alive. The rumors persisted but were largely ignored until a 101-year-old man surfaced named J. Frank Dalton in 1949. Dalton lived near the Meramec Caverns southwest of St. Louis on Route 66, and normally, he would've been a rather uninteresting senior citizen, but he became the center of interest because he claimed to be Jesse James.

Dalton said the assassination was staged as part of an elaborate conspiracy and that the body in the coffin was a man named Charlie Bigelow. He said that Ford murdered Bigelow to claim the bounty, allowing him to leave the area and live out his life under another identity. Jesse's surviving family didn't believe the story. But it should be pointed out that those who knew Jesse best were long dead by 1949 and the only ones alive who knew him were quite young in 1882.

Many thought that the issue would finally be put to rest when the grave of Jesse—or whoever was in the ground under his tombstone—was exhumed in 1995. A DNA sample was taken from the skeletal remains of "Jesse" and subjected to mitochondrial testing. The test showed that the DNA was consistent with a female descendant of Jesse's, which means that the man in the grave was certainly a relative of Jesse James, but not necessarily Jesse himself.

So, it seems that we can all think what we want. The romantics among us like to believe that Jesse James and his friends and family pulled off an elaborate conspiracy allowing him to live out his life as Frank Dalton. The more pragmatic among us tend to believe that, just as Jesse James lived by the gun, he also died by the gun.

A Harbinger of Doom?

From November 12, 1966, to December 15, 1967, the residents of the small town of Point Pleasant, West Virginia were plagued with visitations from what was described as an otherworldly visitor. Witnesses claimed that the creature stood about the same size as an average man and had the body of a man for the most part, with regular arms but claws instead of hands. The creature was also reported to have large, red bug-like eyes and wings that spanned up to ten feet.

The creature was seen running, standing, and flying throughout the countryside around Point Pleasant. It became known as "Mothman." Just as suddenly as Mothman had shown up in Point Pleasant, he disappeared.

But as strange and as frightening as the Mothman sightings were, the people of the area were more concerned about bigger problems on December 15, 1967. On that day, the bridge that connects Point Pleasant to Gallipolis, Ohio via US Highway 35 across the Ohio River—known to locals as the Silver Bridge—collapsed, killing 46 people. The people of the region were still reeling from the tragedy, with many having lost friends and family, and could care less about the sightings of a "monster" out in the country.

But after a few weeks, some began questioning if the appearance of Mothman was a harbinger of some kind. Maybe Mothman was trying to warn the people of Point

Pleasant of the impending doom? Or maybe he was the reason.

The sightings and the possible connection with the bridge collapse became the subject of a 1975 nonfiction book by John Keel titled *The Mothman Prophecies*. In the book, Keel argues that the Mothman was an extraterrestrial visitor who was attempting to warn the residents of the area about the bridge disaster. The idea took hold with many in the community who swear that Mothman is/was real. But, of course, not everyone is convinced.

Skeptics claim that the Mothman sightings in the late 1960s were a combination of misidentification, mass psychosis, and hoaxes. Many of the sightings, critics claim, were probably either large owls or sandhill cranes, while others were hoaxes. Once reports of Mothman sightings began circulating in the area, more and more people began *thinking* they were seeing the legendary creature.

Once the suspension bridge collapsed, which was determined to be a defect in a single link, residents of the area quickly forgot about the Mothman and sightings ceased. But there has been one significant Mothman sighting in recent years.

In 2016, local Charleston, West Virginia television news station WCHS showed video supposedly taken near Point Pleasant of a creature flying above the trees. From many angles, the flying creature certainly appears to have a human-like body, but skeptics say that it is probably just an owl carrying a snake.

Whether the Mothman is real or not, the legend has certainly been good for Point Pleasant. Every year since 2002, the town has held a Mothman Festival that draws more than 10,000 people, proving that perhaps the strange creature was benevolent after all.

It's Really Me

We've all heard about, or seen first-hand, cases of people afflicted with Alzheimer's disease or dementia forgetting their family members' names, or even worse, not being able to recognize their faces. It would be a truly frightening experience to suddenly not be able to recognize your husband or wife in old age, but could you imagine having that problem all your life?

Being a child and not being able to pick your mother's face out from a crowd or not seeing your father in the crowd at one of your sporting events would be both scary and frustrating. You would know something was wrong, but no matter how much you paid attention, all faces would look the same.

About 2% of the population suffers from this rare psychological disorder known as prosopagnosia, where the person with the affliction is "face blind." They are unable, or have extreme difficulty, differentiating people's faces, even those they've known their entire lives. So, what causes prosopagnosia, and can it be treated?

Experts know that prosopagnosia is caused by damage to a fold in the brain known as the right fusiform gyrus. What causes the damage is a bit more complex to understand and relates to the severity or type of prosopagnosia a person has. Stroke, traumatic brain injuries, and congenital disorders can all be potential causes of prosopagnosia, with those who are born with it or develop it early in their lives having some of the greatest difficulties dealing with it, but also having the best potential to overcome it.

Children with prosopagnosia may show signs without describing the problem to their parents directly. For instance, when they are waiting to be picked up at school, they may wait for their parent to wave before going with them. They also may not recognize neighbors or even close family members when they see them away from the neighborhood or home.

If you think you may have prosopagnosia, you can take either the Benton Facial Recognition Test or the Warrington Recognition Memory of Faces Test to check for sure. If you or a loved one are diagnosed with prosopagnosia, unfortunately, there is no cure, although those with the affliction have developed some tricks to help them get by.

Although prosopagnosia is a neurological condition, it doesn't necessarily affect a person's intelligence or memory. Those afflicted with prosopagnosia have developed elaborate memory techniques and mnemonic devices to remember a specific person. They remember a particular person by her haircut or another person by his voice. The reality is that, as rare and bizarre as prosopagnosia is, it isn't debilitating for most people. Apple co-founder Steve Wozniak, Colorado Governor John Hickenlooper, and Victoria, the crown princess of Sweden, all suffer from prosopagnosia.

Foo Fighters

You probably read the title of this chapter and immediately thought of the 1990s rock band, right? Well, our next story in this book has nothing at all to do with this band, other than they got the name from the bizarre phenomenon that took place over the skies of Europe and the Pacific during World War II. Both Axis and Allied soldiers, Marines, pilots, and sailors reported seeing unnaturally fast-moving lights in what were thought to be UFO encounters. American pilots began calling the lights "foo fighters," but the name is less important than what they were.

There is no doubt that something was taking place late in the war, although there is no agreement on what everyone saw. Most believe that the sightings were simply of advanced German rocketry and jets, which were entirely new to the world. Others believe that the foo fighters were even more advanced German and Japanese technology that was never used widely before the end of the war. Of course, others believe foo fighters were not of this world.

The term foo fighter was first used in November 1944 when American pilots in Western Europe claimed to have been chased by red balls of light. With nothing known to compare the lights to, some likened them to the firefighters, known as "foo fighters," in the comic strip *Smokey Stover*. The name began to be used generally for UFOs for the remainder of the war, but there had been numerous UFO sightings throughout the war, in Europe and Asia.

The most immediate explanations were quite terrestrial and logical. The Germans displayed their advanced rocket and jet technology toward the end of the war by launching their V-1 and V-2 rockets at London and sending their jets to fight the allies over Europe. Most scientists believe that since the Allied pilots and men on the ground had never seen rockets or jets before, this alone would've been enough to make imaginations soar. Combined with St. Elmo's fire, some of these rockets and jets must have looked otherworldly.

In the Pacific, the Japanese launched "balloon bombs" toward the end of the war. Balloon bombs were just as the name indicates: incendiary bombs strapped to large helium balloons. But Axis pilots and soldiers on the ground reported these sightings as well. Surely they must've been acquainted enough with their army's weapons, right? Well, here is where we begin to explore some more interesting and alternative theories.

There are several conspiracy theories about this that range in detail, but all pretty much start with the premise that, in addition to rocket and jet technology, the Nazis were experimenting with circular winged aircraft (flying saucers) powered by different, alternative sources of energy. Some variations of this theory hold that the Japanese were also involved in this technology. There are also variations concerning how exactly the Nazis got this technology.

Some of the more mainstream proponents of Nazi flying saucers argue that they had simply arrived at the technology through their rocket and jet experiments, but most say they received it from the stars. Miguel Serrano (remember him?)

even worked the Nazi flying saucers into his Hollow Earth theory (remember that?), by stating that at the end of the war the UFO went to Antarctica and entered the hollow Earth, where they will remain until some point in the future.

The idea of Axis UFOs continued to be brought up from time to time in both the mainstream and UFO communities, but it was largely forgotten until the 1990s. If you were around in the 1990s, then you surely remember the *X-Files*. If you were a fan of that show, then you probably remember Scully and Mulder discussing Nazi flying saucers in at least a couple of episodes.

Just as with all UFO theories, foo fighters remain a mystery. Maybe someday we'll learn what all those people in World War II saw in the skies, but for now, I guess we'll all have to look to the southern sky. Maybe the secrets are in Antarctica. It makes a good story, anyway.

The First Hollywood Scandal

During the 1910s and early 1920s, there wasn't a more recognized actor in America than Roscoe "Fatty" Arbuckle. Known for being able to move across a stage with grace despite his girth, Arbuckle was one of Hollywood's first comedic actors and a true trendsetter.

Born in 1887 in Kansas, Arbuckle grew up in California, where he was exposed to vaudeville acting at an early age. Although young Roscoe never had leading man looks, and he was overweight at a young age, he was mentally sharp and relatively athletic for his size. Arbuckle was able to combine his two talents into a lucrative acting careering by taking roles that few other people could fill (yes, pun intended)!

Arbuckle was one of the original Keystone Cops and became one of Hollywood's first million-dollar actors in 1918. Often billed as "Fatty," Arbuckle became a household name in the 1910s, starring in silent films with the likes of Buster Keaton and Charlie Chaplin. But then everything changed for Fatty during a night of heavy drinking on September 5, 1921. On that night, Arbuckle found himself in the middle of Hollywood's first true scandal.

On September 3, Arbuckle and friends Lowell Sherman and Fred Fishback drove from Los Angeles to San Francisco to spend the Labor Day weekend at the luxurious St. Francis

Hotel. The men invited several young women to attend their party, which included 26-year-old bit actress Virginia Rappe.

Rappe was certainly a beautiful young woman, but she had plenty of baggage and was already quite jaded. She never knew her father, her mother died when she was young, and her fiancé was hit and killed by a streetcar in 1916. She had landed several small roles in the late 1910s and in 1921 seemed destined to be the next starlet of silent film, but Rappe's demons kept getting in the way.

Rappe was a heavy drinker—an alcoholic by today's standards—which contributed to some of her health problems. She had a chronic urinary tract infection that was exacerbated by her drinking, and she was also known to make bad decisions when under the influence of booze.

On the evening of September 5, Rappe drank too much and fell ill, no doubt because of her infection. Arbuckle and the partygoers called a doctor to look at Rappe, who noticed the obvious—she was drunk! The genius doctor then gave her some morphine and told her to pass out. Two days after the party, when Rappe was still sick, she finally checked into a local hospital. Rappe died one day later of a ruptured bladder.

It appeared to the doctor, coroner, and anyone else looking at Virginia Rappe's case that is was all quite simple, yet no doubt tragic. After years of heavy drinking and living a hedonistic lifestyle, it appeared that Rappe's body had finally succumbed. But then Bambina Maude Delmont inserted herself into the case.

Delmont was a friend of Rappe and a bit of a con artist. She was known to extort the rich and famous who found themselves in precarious situations, usually involving sex and/or money. Delmont told the police that Arbuckle had raped Rappe and that his weight must have ruptured her bladder.

Despite Arbuckle's denials that he had any sexual contact with Rappe, and the fact that none of the other witnesses saw Arbuckle assault Rappe in any sort of way, Arbuckle was charged with manslaughter and put on trial.

Justice moved swiftly 100 years ago. Less than two months after he was charged, Arbuckle went on trial in November 1921. It was the crime of the century, at least as far as the media was concerned.

Every major newspaper in America reported on the trial, most with the opinion that Arbuckle was guilty. Despite the lack of evidence, the odds were stacked against Arbuckle. The negative press polluted the minds of the jury, so Arbuckle thought he had to take the stand to defend himself.

The jury deadlocked in December, which resulted in a second trial in January 1922. After another short trial, the second jury also ended in a deadlock. The district attorney decided to go ahead with a third trial, but for Fatty, the third time proved to be a charm. He was acquitted on April 12, 1922. However, his life was all but over.

Arbuckle lost most of his money and property paying his lawyer's fees and he became a *persona non grata* in Hollywood. Even after he was acquitted, most directors were afraid to cast Fatty, and in 1930 new decency guidelines, known as the Hays Code, made it even harder for him.

Although Arbuckle was able to work as a director on some minor projects under a pseudonym, the actor who became wealthy due to his size had taken a major fall from which he was unable to get up.

Fatty died of a heart attack in 1933, at the age of 46. Although hard living and obesity were the prime factors in Arbuckle's early death, there is little doubt that the stress of three manslaughter trials played a contributing role.

Blowing off Some Steam

If you've ever driven through the Upper Peninsula of Michigan or northern Wisconsin or the arrowhead of Minnesota, you may have noticed small structures on the properties of rural homes. There's also a good chance that you didn't notice them because they are so small, but if you did, you may have thought they were outhouses. Some may have been, but most would have been saunas.

Yes, the people of that region of the United States—just like their Finnish ancestors—take saunas very seriously. You've probably spent some time in a sauna. But have you ever considered how culturally important they are to some people, the science behind them, and their health benefits?

Saunas originated in Finland in the Middle Ages and spread from there to the Baltic kingdoms, Scandinavia, Russia, and the German-speaking lands. From those countries, saunas were exported around the world. Today, saunas remain more popular in Europe, but they can be found in nearly every country in the world, in health spas, gyms, and luxury hotels.

Saunas range in size and style, but they are simply a room that is heated by a wood, gas, or electric stove, known as a kiuas. Rocks are then piled on top of the stove to temperatures of more than 200 °F. Normally, such temperatures would be intolerable since that can be high enough to boil water, but the science of saunas allows you to tolerate and even enjoy the

174

temperatures because the air is constantly kept dry. If you want to add some heat and humidity, you just pour a little water over the rocks. Crucially, the wood seating remains cool to the touch: could you imagine sitting on metal in those types of temps?

As simple as the science behind saunas is, the long-lasting health benefits they provide are immense. Finns are among the healthiest and longest-living people in the Western world, which is at least partly due to sauna use. Scientific research has shown that regular sauna bathing is responsible for better cardiovascular health, including lowered blood pressure. Saunas are also good for arthritis, they help detoxify your body, they can help you sleep better, they reduce stress, and they can aid in your recovery from a grueling workout.

On the other hand, those with a history of heart attacks should avoid saunas. But, for most of us, saunas are enjoyable and healthy. So, next time you're feeling stressed and need to blow off some steam, just get naked and jump in a sauna!

How Did Public Enemy #1 Really Die?

In 1934, the United States, much like the rest of the world, was going through some growing pains. It was the middle of the Great Depression, the Dust Bowl had devastated parts of the Plains and Midwest, and organized crime was out of control in some places. About the only good news in 1934 was that prohibition had been repealed at the end of 1933, leaving Americans free to imbibe on booze without the threat of arrest.

Part of the reason for overturning prohibition was because it was so unpopular, but it was also partly to take power away from crime kingpins such as Al Capone. J. Edgar Hoover, the director of the Bureau of Investigation—which would be renamed the Federal Bureau of Investigation in 1935—had some success against the Mafia. By 1934, a new type of criminal became his focus: bank robber gangs.

Gangs led by the likes of Bonnie and Clyde, Machine Gun Kelly, and John Dillinger cut across the South and Midwest with their souped-up coupes, Thompson submachine guns, and plenty of attitude, taking down scores and often leaving bodies in their wake. By 1934, Hoover put John Dillinger at the top of his list as "Public Enemy #1," and less than a year later, Dillinger was shot to death outside a movie theater in Chicago, Illinois. Or was he?

176

We know for sure that John Dillinger's story began when he was born on June 22, 1903, in Indianapolis, Indiana. Young Johnny was a troublemaker from the start, fighting, stealing, and drinking when other kids were still playing with toys. Dillinger eventually began getting arrested, which led him to join the Navy. But the Navy just wasn't for a rule breaker like Dillinger. He was dishonorably discharged and returned to Indiana.

Dillinger tried to fit in with "square" society by marrying and working some low-paying jobs, but the thrill and lure of riches drew him back into the criminal lifestyle. After a failed robbery, Dillinger was sent to state prison in 1924, which is where he remained until 1933.

Prison made Dillinger an angry young man, but it also allowed him to make some connections and hone his criminal skills. Naturally charismatic and street, if not book, smart Dillinger formed a gang behind bars and planned to bring his act on the road when he was released. Dillinger and his associates robbed banks throughout the Midwest and were careful to always keep moving.

They had hideouts in Indiana, Minnesota, and Illinois. If the heat got to be too much in one location, they simply moved to the next spot. But by late 1933, the heat was becoming too much everywhere, and the full force of the federal government and J. Edgar Hoover were coming down on Dillinger. After Dillinger and some of his guys were arrested in Arizona in January 1934, he was transferred to Crown Point, Indiana, where he promptly escaped. The escape made Dillinger Public Enemy #1, and at that point, his fate was sealed.

Dillinger's escape made the FBI and Hoover look bad, and he surely relished the experience. Dillinger had some minor plastic surgery done to alter his appearance, but he was the type of guy who needed to be in the limelight. He liked to drink, he enjoyed the company of women and, most importantly, he desired to be the center of attention. When he met a teenage runaway named Polly Hamilton in June 1934, all of those qualities came together to conspire against Dillinger.

Hamilton knew Dillinger as "Jimmy Lawrence," which she never questioned, but her friend, Romanian immigrant brothel owner Ana Cumpănaş, noticed that the man looked an awful lot like Dillinger. Cumpănaş decided to contact the FBI. Cumpănaş wanted to cash in on the reward, but her goal was primarily to stop deportation proceedings against her. When the FBI told her they could help, Cumpănaş agreed to serve Dillinger up to them on the evening of July 22.

When Dillinger left the theater with Hamilton and Cumpănaş just after 10:30 p.m., an FBI team was waiting for him on the street. When FBI agent Melvin Purvis identified Dillinger, he lit a cigar, which was the signal for the takedown. Dillinger ran into an alley and shot three agents, who returned fire, shooting and killing Dillinger. Or at least this is the official story. From this point on, the story gets a little strange.

Dillinger's father came to Chicago to identify the corpse, which he refused to do, saying it wasn't his son. Then there were numerous anomalies in the coroner's report. The corpse supposedly had brown eyes, while Dillinger was known to have baby blues. The body lacked scars Dillinger was known to have, although he may have had them removed when he got plastic surgery. Most notably, the body was much shorter than Dillinger's known height. The body on the examination table had also suffered from a life of rheumatic heart condition, which would've kept Dillinger out of the Navy. Also, Dillinger was not known to have any major health problems.

In 1963, someone claiming to be Dillinger wrote a letter to the *Indianapolis Star*. Well into the 1980s, there were Dillinger sightings throughout the world. Some of the sightings had him in Oregon, Washington, or California, while others placed him in more exotic locales such as Brazil and Argentina. In all of these scenarios, Dillinger died of old age, presumably living off his ill-gotten earnings.

So, if Dillinger wasn't gunned down outside the theater in Chicago, who was the man on the autopsy table? The best guess would be that it was one of his crew members, but it would be difficult to say. Since Dillinger has living relatives and the body of the man suspected of being him was buried in Crown Point, Indiana, all of the controversies could be cleared up with a DNA test. However, the cemetery owners haven't permitted his body to be exhumed. It appears this is a conspiracy theory that won't go away anytime soon.

The World's Oldest Profession

In case you didn't know, it is often said that prostitution, or sex work as it's now known, is the world's oldest profession. The implication is that women, and occasionally men, have always traded the use of their bodies to others for money or other goods. A closer look reveals that although sex work is certainly one of the oldest professions, it is probably not *the* oldest profession known to man or woman.

Referring to sex work as the oldest profession is a pretty recent phenomenon that was started by British writer Rudyard Kipling in his 1888 book *On the City Wall*. Since that time, it has been used extensively throughout the world, but how true is it?

When humans began emerging from the last Ice Age just over 10,000 years ago, sex was important but primarily for procreation reasons. There were no true professions to speak of during this period, although the skills most in-demand in tribes were hunting, fighting, and the ability to make various tools. It wasn't until the Neolithic Period when tribes began merging and creating towns and other permanent settlements that professions/trades began forming.

The earliest trades in the Neolithic Period were craftsmen (tool makers), farmers, warriors, merchants, and priests. Since humans had yet to invent/discover writing in the Neolithic Period, there is no evidence for sex work in this period, although that doesn't mean it didn't exist. The first evidence for sex work in history comes after the first true civilizations formed after 3,100 BCE. Settlements evolved into cities in Egypt, Mesopotamia, and the Levant (roughly equivalent to the modern countries of Israel, Lebanon, and coastal Syria) and all of a sudden plenty of people had disposable incomes.

Men could indulge their desires outside of or as a substitute to marriage. You may be surprised to know, however, that many early sex workers were temple priestesses. Yes, you read that correctly, many of the sex workers in the Bronze Age Near East (3000–1200 BCE) were sanctioned by the religious authorities!

In places like Ugarit on the Mediterranean coast and in the Mesopotamian cities of Babylon, Uruk, and Ur, sex workers were known to use their craft to make a little money for the temple. After the Bronze Age, sex work was formalized to a certain degree and was tolerated by various cultures throughout the world into modern times.

So, sex work is indeed an old profession that has been practiced for thousands of years, but it technically isn't the oldest profession. Sex work is only as old as organized civilization when the combination of legal and economic order and stability allowed such an activity to flourish. Before that time, sex was almost entirely done for procreative reasons. And before that time, men were more worried about defending themselves from saber tooth tigers and finding enough to eat than they were about getting a little extra nooky behind the cave!

A New Insect Problem

In a previous volume of *Interesting Stories*, we discussed how killer bees have made their way north from Brazil to the United States. Although they've created problems for some beekeepers, they haven't necessarily lived up to their name. Yes, they can be quite deadly to those with allergies to bee stings, but they have not turned out to be the apocalyptic force that cheesy 1970s movies portrayed them as. In this volume, we looked at the fire ant invasion. Again, the fire ants have caused some problems in the Southern states, but nothing that can't be overcome.

Now we have a new entrant into the insect invasion sweepstakes. This contestant is much bigger than the other two and has the scariest name—murder hornets. Yes, these hornets aren't just inadvertently killing some things that get in their way as killer bees do. No, murder hornets set out with the clear intent of first-degree murder.

Well, not exactly. Murder hornets are Asian giant hornets (*Vespa mandarinia*), and although they are quite big—almost two inches long on average with a three-inch wingspan— there is no evidence that these insects are committing premeditated murders. With that said, this large, invasive insect species recently began cropping up in the Pacific Northwest of North America, so it is important to know what they are capable of. The moniker "murder hornet" is more hype than fact. Yes, if you have certain allergies, you should be aware of these large insects, but you should even around honeybees. It turns out that murder hornets kill about 40 people a year in all of Asia, primarily in Japan, compared to around 80 people who die from bee stings annually in the United States.

If you do get stung by a murder hornet, though, you'll be sure to remember it. The sting is more powerful and the venom more toxic than other bee stings, which keeps people away from these bugs more than anything. Murder hornets also tend to build their colonies underground, so humans generally don't come into extensive contact with them.

But what about the interaction between murder hornets and other animals in North America? Scientists and farmers are most worried about murder hornets overrunning honeybee colonies and apiaries. It turns out that murder hornets have a talent for killing bees and taking their honey, so experts are keeping their eyes on the honeybee population of the Northwest. So far, there isn't any evidence that murder hornets are invading the honeybees, but the animal kingdom can be an unpredictable place. Let's just hope that this new insect problem doesn't hurt our honey supply.

Immunity to HIV?

When acquired immune deficiency syndrome (AIDS), and the linked disease human immunodeficiency virus infection (HIV), were first identified in the 1980s, they were believed to be a death sentence for anyone who acquired them. Patients with HIV/AIDS often suffered long and agonizing illnesses before succumbing to the disease. After one was infected, symptoms could show within weeks to months, and death was almost assured within five years.

But by the early 1990s, advances in medical science meant that new drugs could keep HIV/AIDS patients alive for many more years; indefinitely if they lived a generally healthy lifestyle. The new scientific advances in HIV/AIDS treatment weren't just focused on treatment, though.

In 1994, a man named Stephen Crohn came to the scientific and medical establishments' attention when it was revealed that he'd had unprotected sex with several male partners who had tested positive for HIV/AIDS. A battery of tests was run on Crohn until they discovered that his apparent immunity to the deadly disease probably had something to do with a genetic mutation.

HIV/AIDS is a virus that destroys the white blood cells in the human body. Once enough white blood cells are destroyed, then the body is susceptible to several diseases, which is how HIV/AIDS patients die. In Crohn's case, scientists determined that a mutation he had called "delta 32" prevented the virus from taking hold of his body. Further research has shown that up to 10% of the Caucasian population in the world may have the delta-32 mutation, and therefore, is immune to HIV/AIDS.

More recent studies have indicated that humans also have other natural defenses against HIV/AIDS. A study of sex workers in Kenya showed that some people can develop an immunity to HIV/AIDS despite not having the delta-32 mutation.

The sex workers in question had repeated unprotected HIV/AIDS positive clients yet did not contract the virus. Some of the same sex workers who had avoided contracting HIV/AIDS, though, later did contract the virus after abstaining from sexual contact with infected persons for a certain period.

The somewhat baffling results led researches to believe that the body can build a natural defense to HIV/AIDS when it has repeated contact with the virus. Researchers identified what are known as cytotoxic T lymphocytes (CTLs) as being activated when the body is under repeated exposure to HIV/AIDS. When the exposure to HIV/AIDS ends or is severely reduced, the body quits making CTLs.

So, what does all this mean? It certainly doesn't mean that you have carte blanche to engage in risky activity, but it does mean that there is always hope. Perhaps most importantly, it's a good example of just how little we know. When we think we have something figured out—BAM!—we get hit with something that shows we need to look in a different direction.

The Man Who Wouldn't Die

Grigori Rasputin was born in a small village in the wilds of Siberia in 1869. There was nothing spectacular about Rasputin's background that would suggest he'd play an important role in history or that he'd die a most spectacular death. He married a fellow peasant woman and had a small family, living on the soil of Siberia. But then, in 1897, Rasputin had a mystical revelation.

He left his home for some time and learned to read and write at a Russian Orthodox monastery. Rasputin claimed to have had visions and so dedicated his life to a newfound spiritual and mystical path. He traveled throughout Russia and possibly other Eastern European countries for several years, eventually ending up in St. Petersburg by 1905.

In 1905, St. Petersburg was the heart of Russia. It was the location of the royal palace, where Tsar Nicholas II Romanov and his family spent most of their time. The Romanovs lived in opulence, seemingly unaware that their nation was collapsing around them. The peasants were poor, and the urban workers were angry. They became increasingly organized by the anarchists and communists. For Nicholas, though, the only thing that mattered was his son, the Crown Prince Alexei. Alexei suffered from hemophilia, which 100 years ago often meant a short life, and certainly one filled with pain.

As the tsar hosted lavish parties in the Winter Palace, a strange bearded man from Siberia made his rounds. If there's one thing that rich people anywhere like, it's an eccentric who can entertain the crowd with stories. As the tsar listened to people talk about the bearded eccentric, he learned that the man's name was Rasputin and that he was a mystic who had powers. The tsar was immediately impressed, and within a short time, Rasputin became Alexei's faith healer.

The Romanov's believed Rasputin was healing their son, so they brought him closer into their inner circle, which was a dangerous place to be. Once World War I began, the tsar went to the front with the troops, which left Rasputin alone with the tsarina and the Romanov children. Rumors immediately began circulating that Rasputin was having an affair with the tsarina and that he was the true power behind the throne. There is no evidence of any of this, but it didn't stop disaffected nobles, clergy and members of the Church hierarchy, and communists from spreading the rumor.

Once World War I began, Rasputin was living on borrowed time. The first attempt on Rasputin's life came on July 12, 1914, when he was stabbed in the stomach near his Siberian home by a woman who was part of a rival religious sect. Although Rasputin was severely injured and spent considerable time recovering, he was back in St. Petersburg by 1915. It would take much more than a mere stabbing to kill Rasputin!

Things were not going well for the royals in Russia in late 1916. They were losing battle after battle to the Germans and Austrians and the communists were organizing protests in factories and protests on the streets of Moscow, St. Petersburg, and other major Russian cities. For whatever reason, the nobles, who supported the war effort and the monarchy, if not Nicholas II specifically, blamed Rasputin for Russia's problems. In their eyes, Rasputin had to die.

Felix Yusupov, who was married to one of the tsar's nieces, invited Rasputin to his St. Petersburg home just after midnight under the guise that they would discuss some theological matters. Yusupov first offered Rasputin some cyanide-laced tea and cake, but when that didn't work, Yusupov had to move on to Plan B, which was poisoned wine. After two hours of drinking, with the poison having no apparent effect, he shot Rasputin in the chest.

Yusupov and some of the other conspirators then cleaned up the scene and went to Rasputin's apartment to make it look as though he was home, but when they returned to Yusupov's place, they were greeted with a surprise. Rasputin rose, seemingly from the dead, and attacked Yusupov, with a bloody brawl ensuing. The other conspirators finally got a hold of themselves and finished Rasputin off with two more shots. At least one of the conspirators also stabbed him a few times in the face for good measure.

They then dumped his body in a nearby river. Rasputin's body was discovered the next day, and almost immediately, he became a legend. He became known as the monk who wouldn't die, and for that reason, the communists burned his body when they came to power.

Now That's Reinventing Yourself!

In 1963, Alabama governor-elect George Wallace gave an inaugural speech in front of the state capitol in Montgomery that truly fired up his base. He railed against the civil rights movement and leading figures in it such as Martin Luther King Jr. Once he had the crowd whipped up into a frenzy, he proclaimed, "Segregation now, segregation tomorrow, segregation forever!"

You can say what you want about the content of the speech, but you must admit it was well-written. You'd probably not be surprised that the speech was written by a militant segregationist who started his own paramilitary Ku Klux Klan group. But you probably *would* be surprised to learn that the speech's author also wrote the 1972 novel, *The Rebel Outlaw: Josey Wales*. If you aren't familiar with that book, it was turned into the 1976 blockbuster film, *The Outlaw Josey Wales* starring Clint Eastwood. The author of Wallace's speech and *Josey Wales* was a man named Asa Earl Carter. Carter's sometimes violent and strange life was controversial and confusing to many. However, it is a testament to all that, if you put your mind to it, you can reinvent yourself in America.

Asa Carter was born in segregated Alabama in 1925. He grew up in the height of the Jim Crow era, not only passively accepting the South's racial ideas of the period but becoming a major advocate for them in his adulthood. After serving in the

189

Navy in World War II, Carter returned to Alabama and jumped headfirst into the pro-segregationist movement. Carter worked as a radio deejay in the 1950s, where he regularly shouted invectives against Blacks, Jews, and Whites who supported integration.

But Carter was even too radical for most people in Alabama at the time, so he lost the gig. It proved to be only a minor setback for a man who was constantly reinventing himself according to the situation and the time in which he found himself. After helping to organize segregationists, Carter decided to form a new, more radical Klan group in 1957, which he called the Original Ku Klux Klan of the Confederacy. Carter's Klan was violent, leading to numerous scrapes with the normally pro-segregation police in Alabama.

By the late 1950s, though, Carter found that his true talents weren't in organizing or street fighting but writing. Carter discovered he had a true talent with words and was able to use that talent to make a living while continuing to promote his segregationist ideas by working with Wallace. The two had a falling out, though, when Wallace decided to moderate his message on race in the late '60s.

With the cause of segregation over by the 1970s, Carter disappeared from the face of the Earth. Well, Asa Earl Carter disappeared, and Forrest Carter was reborn. Not wanting to be connected to his militant segregationist Klansman past, Carter changed his first name. He consciously kept a connection though because "Forrest" was chosen after the Confederate war hero and founder of the original Ku Klux Klan, Nathan Bedford Forrest.

Carter moved back and forth from Texas and Florida, avoiding his old friends, and not having anything to do with politics. Carter began writing fictional books about Cherokee Indians and culture. He told his new friends and acquaintances that he was part Cherokee and was raised in a log cabin in Tennessee. No one had any reason to doubt him. Carter did have a dark complexion and, after all, why would anyone lie about such things?

Carter's books started to sell, and by the mid-1970s, he had become a successful, respected author. He was even interviewed by Barbara Walters on the *Today* show in 1975. But with fame comes scrutiny. Even in the pre-Internet 1970s, a secret as big as Carter's was bound to eventually become public. As Carter was riding the wave of his fame, a 1976 *New York Times* article written by an Alabama reporter who knew segregationist Asa Carter spilled the beans.

Despite the news, the movie *The Outlaw Josie Wales* became a big hit in 1976, and Carter's *The Education of Little Tree* came out in 1976 describing his life with a Cherokee family. Even after *Little Tree* was revealed not to be an autobiography, it was still a bestseller and was turned into a 1997 film of the same name.

Carter died of a heart attack in 1979 at his home in Abilene, Texas. Opinions on him as a person and his life's work are mixed. Chuck Weeth, one of Carter's friends in Texas who knew nothing about his Klansman past said, "I didn't like Asa Carter, but I did like Forrest Carter." We can never truly know what's in a person's heart and mind, but there is little doubt that Asa Carter attempted one of the more radical personal rebrandings in history.

The B1 Butcher

Namibia's B1 is the country's most important highway. Stretching from the southern border with South Africa to the northern border with Angola, the B1 highway goes through nearly 1,000 miles of Namibia, through deserts, over mountains, and through some of the country's largest cities, including Windhoek.

Since construction first began on the B1 in the 1950s, it's been known as one of the deadliest roads in Africa. Multi-car accidents are frequent on some sections of the highway and there is always the chance that wild or domestic animals can cause an accident. In the mid-2000s, though, the people of Namibia were worrying about being the victim of a different kind of animal on the B1 highway.

Beginning in 2005, body parts of women in plastic bags began turning up near the B1 highway in the area around the city of Windhoek. The murders weren't even connected until 2007 when the total was five. The victims were determined to have been murdered in different ways, with most being strangled, though at least one victim was beaten to death.

The difference in murder methods kept investigators from originally linking the crimes, but the fact that they were all dismembered pointed in that direction. Then there was the fact that all of the body parts showed signs of being stored in a freezer. Finally, all of the victims were young women of Namibian Colored ethnicity.

The investigators realized that they had a serial killer on their hands who was using the B1 highway as his dumping ground. Capturing him would be no easy task. Since at least two of the victims were sex workers, the police scoured their informants in the sex worker world for information, but they were unsuccessful.

Then the case took another strange twist when someone claiming to be the killer sent a taunting letter to the police. Although the letter didn't immediately have an impact on the case, it did later play a role. The first major break came, as they often do in similar cases, through chance.

Forty-two-year-old German citizen Heinz Knierim was arrested for the rape of a young Colored woman in the Windhoek area in August 2007. The more the police looked at Knierim, the more he looked good for the B1 murders. He couldn't account for his movements during many of the murders and he fit the profile. Yet there was a lack of evidence tying Knierim to any of the crimes, which led to his acquittal in 2010.

But, as Knierim was awaiting trial, another suspect came to the police's attention. Hans Husselmann was a career criminal who had served most of his adult life in prison for two murders. After he was released in 2004, Husselmann never seemed to find stability, drifting around the Windhoek area until he killed himself in 2008.

The police later revealed that DNA from one of the victims was found in Husselmann's apartment and that his DNA tied him to the letter sent to the police. But does that mean that Husselmann was the killer? The truth is that most of the B1

Butcher's victims were sex workers, so the fact that DNA from one of the victims was found in Husselmann's apartment is not proof of anything other than a connection. The fact that he wrote the letter certainly doesn't look good, though.

It appears that the very specific types of murders attributed to the B1 Butcher have stopped, although he could've changed his MO. He could still be out there killing but disposing of his victims differently. Namibia is a large country with a lot of empty, vast space. Perhaps the B1 Killer has been making trips to the hills or deserts near Windhoek. The reality is that we'll probably never know who the B1 Butcher is.

Peanuts Sure Can
Pack a Punch

For most people in the world, peanuts are a harmless snack that can help kill food cravings, but for about 3% of the population in the Western world, they can kill. Unless you are plagued with a peanut allergy, it may be difficult to believe that these delectable little morsels are the number one cause of food anaphylaxis in the world—severe swelling resulting from an allergic reaction. And if not treated quickly, anaphylaxis can lead to death.

So, why are some people afflicted with peanut allergies while most of us aren't? As with allergies in general, it is difficult to pinpoint what causes a person to have a peanut allergy. Most people develop a peanut allergy at a young age or are born with it, which suggests a genetic propensity in some cases. Allergies to other foods, such as shellfish, may also indicate a potential peanut allergy, and those with eczema may also be susceptible to a peanut allergy.

Although doctors and scientists may not understand the root causes of a peanut allergy, they know what can trigger an attack. Eating food with peanuts, or even something only lightly cross-contaminated with peanuts, can result in an attack. For those with a severe peanut allergy, even touching or breathing in peanut dust can cause anaphylaxis.

So, what's a peanut allergy sufferer to do? Well, about all you can do is stay far away from peanuts and if an attack does occur, seek medical attention. But there is something you can do to prevent your young children from developing a peanut allergy.

Although it may seem counterintuitive, in 2015, the American Academy of Pediatrics began recommending that parents with infants at high risk of developing a peanut allergy should *give* their children peanut butter and other peanut-based foods. This went against the long-held belief that parents should avoid giving their children any peanut-based foods. Sometimes, with time, comes a better understanding of science.

Studies have indicated that children who are given small amounts of peanut butter develop immunity to peanut allergy. The experts recommend not giving a child at risk to peanut allergy peanut butter or any other peanut based food until you talk to your doctor. But if the doctor says, "go ahead," I'm sure your little ones will love it!

What's in a Name?

Just about everywhere you go in the world today, people have surnames. How they are used varies slightly from culture to culture: the surname comes first in many east Asian countries and in Spanish-speaking countries, people carry two surnames for both sides of their families. But the idea is the same—a surname is simply the name we inherit from our fathers, or sometimes, from our mothers.

Today, surnames are used by everyone except rich and famous people who feel privileged and eccentric enough to go by only one name. The modern concept of surnames is not very old, but simultaneously is also based on some very ancient ideas. The ancient Egyptians were among the first people in recorded history to use more than one name. The pharaohs were known by five different names, although their fifth name was the name they used day-to-day and what we know them by today.

Likewise, non-royal Egyptians were generally only known by one name, but they would sometimes include their genealogy as part of their name in some texts. For instance, a scribe named Nefer was the son of Paneb, so he may have been known as "Nefer Son of Paneb," or even "Nefer Paneb." Like the Egyptians, the Greeks were generally just known by their first name, although some of the better-known Greek philosophers, scientists, and historians often added their home or place of birth. Herodotus, the "father of history," was commonly known as "Herodotus of Halicarnassus."

The Romans later institutionalized the ideas of surnames that were first used by the Egyptians and Greeks and expanded on them. At the height of the Roman Empire, Roman names could be quite long and sometimes difficult to pronounce. In addition to the family and given name, Romans could also add names to signify certain accomplishments. Remember Scipio earlier in this book? His full name was Publius Cornelius Scipio Africanus. Scipio was the name of the branch of his family and Cornelia was their clan. His father's name was Publius, so he was junior, and he earned the name "Africanus" after defeating Hannibal.

Surnames fell out of favor after the Roman Empire collapsed and didn't become popular again until the 1500s and 1600s throughout Europe. The advent of modern record-keeping and taxation mandated that people have surnames to keep track of them. The next step was for people to give themselves surnames.

Many people simply took the name of their occupations. Carpenters, Taylors, Bakers, and Coopers (barrel makers) became common in Britain, while Beckers (baker), Schmidts (smith), and Metzs (butcher) became common in the German-speaking countries. Toponyms (geography) also became quite popular sources for surnames. This naming tradition led to plenty of people named Rome, Navarro (after the Kingdom of Navarre in northern Spain), and Berlin.

If all else failed, you just took your father's first name as your last and added "son." This style of surname was most popular in Scandinavia and also became popular in Scotland and other parts of Britain influenced by Scandinavians. In Iceland, the tradition was gender specific. For example, the son may have been named "Hakon Olafson," while the daughter would've been "Ingrid Olafsdottar."

So, now you can look at your name and those of your friends and family and possibly tell a little bit about their backgrounds. If you have a friend named "Schutz," their forebearers may have worked to protect a king or other notable person; someone named "Castile" has ancestors from that part of Spain; and if your friend is named "Erickson," then they are probably descended from some Vikings.

Of course, there are also some strange surnames. If you meet someone named "Spinster," then somewhere along the line, they had an ancestor who quit being one, the name "Strange" is itself not so rare and originated in France, and "Fuchs" is a German name that probably relates to the originator hunting fox, or being as crafty as one … not what you probably thought at first!

The Original LA Confidential

On the morning of January 15, 1947, the mangled body of 22-year-old Elizabeth Short was found in a vacant lot of the Leimert Park neighborhood of Los Angeles, California. Well, mangled is quite an understatement. Short's body had been eviscerated and torn into two. It was like nothing the police had seen before and when the medical examiner gave the body a more thorough examination, it was even worse.

Short's body was severed at the waist and drained of blood, which meant that she was killed at a different location. Her face was cut ear to ear, her guts were taken out and put under her buttocks, and her legs were spread in a pose. She was determined to have died from the slashes to her face and head that caused a cerebral hemorrhage. Although no semen was found on the body, it appeared she was probably anally raped. The killer had made sure to cover his tracks by wiping the body parts down with gasoline to eliminate fingerprints.

Los Angeles had recently experienced an upsurge in organized crime, but what the police had in front of them that morning was like nothing they'd seen before; it was like nothing seen before in the United States, for that matter. This case would attract worldwide attention, becoming known as the "Black Dahlia Murder."

Short become known as the Black Dahlia after her murder, but the origins of the term remain a mystery. Much of the Black

Dahlia case remains a mystery. There was no shortage of suspects in the gruesome crime, yet an arrest was never made. The police were baffled from the start. They had no leads to begin with, so they began by looking at Short's background.

Elizabeth Short was an attractive young woman with blue eyes and dark brown hair. Unfortunately, her looks were about the only positive thing in her short and disappointing life. Short was born and raised in Boston, Massachusetts, but almost from the beginning, it was apparent that she was going to have a tough life.

Her father abandoned the family when she was just six, but instead of leaving with a goodbye note or running off with another woman, he parked his car on a bridge, apparently to make it appear that he had committed suicide. Years later, when Elizabeth was a young adult, he was found to be very much alive and living in Los Angeles.

Elizabeth was also plagued with health problems from an early age, suffering from severe asthma. The condition forced her to spend winters in Florida with relatives and the rest of the year in Boston. The constant moving and instability prevented Elizabeth graduating from high school.

When Elizabeth found out that her father was still alive and living in Los Angeles, she went out there to live with him, hoping that the weather would be good for her health and that maybe she could renew her relationship with him. The father-daughter reunion was short-lived, though, as Elizabeth decided to move out of his house.

Short worked as a waitress and, like most young women living in Los Angeles, had dreams of Hollywood. As she worked and barhopped around LA, she met an Army pilot who proposed marriage. Although Elizabeth accepted the proposal, she continued to be a party girl after her beau shipped off to the Pacific. Then Elizabeth's poor luck came back to haunt her.

First, she was arrested in LA in 1943 for underage drinking. She was supposed to go back to her mother's in Boston but went to Florida instead. Then she found out that her pilot fiancé had died in the Pacific less than a week before the end of World War II. Elizabeth spent the next year and a half on the LA party scene with different lovers, many with shady reputations.

Based on interviews from her known associates, the police were able to piece together the last hours of the Black Dahlia's life. On January 9, 1947, Short returned to Los Angeles from a trip to San Diego with a 25-year-old married man named Robert Manley. She went to her hotel and then to a bar down the street, which was the last place and time she was seen alive. The police believe either she met her killer at the bar, or she called from there and met him somewhere else. Short almost certainly knew her killer.

The first break in the investigation came on January 24, when a package addressed to the *Los Angeles Examiner* was intercepted by a postal worker. The package contained a letter made from letters cut and pasted from newspapers that said, "Here is Dahlia's belongings. Letter to follow." Included in the package were her birth certificate, pictures, photo cards, and an address book with "Mark Hansen" on the front. It had also been wiped with gasoline.

The focus of the investigation was initially on Mark Hansen, who the police learned was a wealthy nightclub owner. He had supposedly been rebuffed by Short, but his alibi checked out, as did Robert Manley's. It turns out he had gone straight home to his wife. Both men were cleared, but it quickly turned out that there was no shortage of suspects. If anything, there were *too many* suspects.

The next promising lead came when a handwritten note was sent to the *Examiner* on January 26 that read "Here it is. Turning in Wed., Jan. 29, 10 am. Had my fun at police. Black Dahlia Avenger." The letter also gave the police a time and place to meet, but the author never showed. The *Examiner* then received another cut and paste letter that said, "Have changed my mind. You would not give me a square deal. Dahlia killing was justified."

In the decades since the Black Dahlia murder, more than 500 people have confessed to the crime. Nearly all have been ruled out, but there were some good suspects. At the top of the list was Walter Bayley. He was a surgeon who lived a block away and had a daughter who was friends with Short's sister. Bayley certainly had the medical background for the amputation, but there is a lack of motive.

Another potential suspect was 27-year-old bellhop Leslie Dillon. Dillon had a morbid fascination with murder and mayhem and injected himself into the case when he wrote a letter to a true-crime writer claiming to know the killer. Other theories are that the Black Dahlia was the victim of crime lord Bugsy Siegel or that she was possibly the victim of the Cleveland Torso Murders killer, who terrorized that city from 1935 to 1938. One of the more interesting theories was put forward by LAPD homicide detective Steve Hodel. He claimed that his father, George Hodel, confessed to the crime and boasted that he'd never get caught.

Although the killer, or killers, of Elizabeth Short are certainly now deceased, there are still many crime writers and detectives who work on the case in their spare time. Who knows, maybe one day that definitive piece of evidence will be found that will finally close the book on the mysterious Black Dahlia murder.

That Really Sucks

The medical profession has advanced quite a bit over the last 100 years. If you think about it, the use of leeches to bleed patients of toxins and other diseased elements was still a regular practice throughout the 1800s. Antibiotic medicine wasn't discovered until the early 1900s, so before that time, there was a lot of trial and error, which often involved amputation of limbs.

But as new technology and medicines are discovered, some people prefer to use older, "alternative" treatments. Cupping is one such procedure. As the name indicates, cupping involves placing cups on a patient's body to reduce inflammation and increase blood flow. The ancient Egyptians practiced variations of cupping and cupping was attempted to save William Henry Harrison. So, how does cupping work and is it effective?

Cupping is a pretty simple and inexpensive process, which is partially why it's still popular in parts of east Asia and Latin America. Also, people who use cupping swear by its efficacy. A cupping procedure is performed by a specialist who has the patient either sit in a chair or lie down on a table. The specialist then takes a cup—or cups—made of bamboo, glass, earthenware, or silicone and burns a substance in it/them. The specialist then applies the cup(s) to the patient. As the cup cools down, it draws the skin up, creating a bulge.

If the specialist is using the dry method, they simply remove the cup after about three minutes. If the specialist is using the wet method, they apply small cuts with a scalpel. Similar to the wet method, some specialists also apply acupuncture needles first and then the cups are applied over the needles.

So, what does cupping do? A 2015 article in the *Journal of Traditional and Complementary Medicine* reports that studies show cupping may help alleviate acne, herpes, and general pain. Although many doctors and scientists remain skeptical of cupping, they point out that it is relatively safe. Those who swear by cupping will tell you that, although it sucks, it has helped make their lives better!

The Paralyzed Woman and the Deaf Man

On May 21, 1960, a 7.6 magnitude earthquake got the attention of the people of Valdivia, Chile, but it was just an ominous sign of things to come. The next day a massive 9.5 earthquake hit Chile, killing thousands, and setting off a series of events that were tragic, inspirational and, some would say, supernatural.

As with most earthquakes that at least partially happen in the ocean, this one caused a major tsunami. After forming off the coast of Chile, the tsunami moved north and west at incredible speeds, striking the west coast of the United States. It did the most damage, however, to what was at the time the new state of Hawaii.

On May 23, the tsunami was bearing down on the Aloha State. The Pacific Tsunami Warning System gave the people of Hawaii six hours to move away from the coast to higher ground, which, for the most part, proved to be effective. Sixty-one people died when they refused to evacuate Hilo Bay, but the more populated Oahu and the city of Honolulu were spared because everyone evacuated. It also helped that the wave didn't hit Oahu until two days later.

When the people of Hawaii began cleaning up after the disaster, reports of heroism and self-sacrifice began to circulate. One story had a potentially supernatural tinge to it and became the subject of a season three episode of the American television series *One Step Beyond* titled "Tidalwave".

Margaret North and her husband had just moved to Honolulu from the mainland. Margaret was confined to a wheelchair due to polio and had yet to meet any of her neighbors. Against his better judgment, Merit North went to work that day for the Navy, at the other end of the island. When Merit heard about the approaching wave, he attempted to call his wife, but he couldn't reach her.

Miles away from Margaret was Thomas A. Powers, a retired naval commander who was visiting Honolulu. He was deaf and a bit on the stubborn side. He decided to drive into Honolulu to visit the beach just as the wave approached.

As the sirens blared, Margaret grew frantic, but Thomas obliviously drove closer to the shore. He didn't hear the sirens or radio reports and with each minute was driving closer to his death. Since Thomas didn't know the city, and since it was an era long before GPS, he became lost.

Margaret knew that she was running out of time so, in desperation, she got out of her wheelchair and tried to make it to the street. She fell behind her home's fence where no one could see her. She screamed for help, but no one was there to hear. Or was someone there?

In what can only be described as a miracle, Thomas just happened to be driving by the North home when he heard a woman cry. Yes, he claimed he heard Margaret North crying for help. He walked up to the North's fence and found Margret on the ground. She then broke the news to him that they were about to be overcome by a tidal wave.

North later said that she believed the experience was a genuine psychic experience. Perhaps these types of experiences happen quite often, but we just aren't paying attention to what the cosmos is telling us.

Will the Real Black Bart Please Step Forward?

Many of the world's greatest outlaws and criminals are known by clever nicknames and easily recognizable monikers. For example, you probably don't know who Harry Longabaugh is offhand because you know him better as the Sundance Kid. Most notorious outlaws acquired their nicknames through a combination of their deeds and their real names, while others picked theirs up due to their physical features.

Sometimes more than one notorious criminal has the same nickname. Charles "Lucky" Luciano and Alphonse Capone were both known as "Scarface" due to wounds they received in their long and dangerous criminal careers. Another nickname that was used by more than one notorious outlaw was "Black Bart."

Unlike the two Scarfaces, who were contemporaries and worked with each other, the two men named Black Bart were separated by more than 100 years and thousands of miles.

The first major outlaw to be known as Black Bart was born John Roberts in Wales in 1682. Little is known about his early life; however, it's certain that, by 1718, he was a second mate on a slave ship. Life was good for Roberts until his ship was captured by two pirate ships off the coast of Africa. The pirates gave Roberts an offer he couldn't refuse: join or die!

Roberts, of course, chose to live and joined the pirates. Within a short time, he was raiding ships off the coast of Africa and in the Caribbean. The captain of the pirate ship was a fellow Welshman, which helped Roberts rise quickly through the ranks of the pirate world.

Before too long, he changed his first name to Bartholomew, and his often-violent deeds became known throughout the British, French, and Spanish empires. He acquired plenty of enemies as well.

Roberts was soon in command of a sizable pirate force and was raiding spots from the Antilles to Canada and from Mexico to Africa. After a short but brilliant career as a pirate, Roberts was killed by a canon from a British ship off the African coast in 1722. In death, Robert's reputation grew into a legend, though it wasn't until much later that he became known as "Black Bart."

The second Black Bart is probably the one best known to Americans. Charles Boles, later known as Charles Bolton, was born in England in 1829 but raised in the United States. Young Charles led an exciting life and was quite well-traveled for the time.

When he was about 20, he went to California to take part in the Gold Rush, but like so many of the other young men, instead of striking it rich, he struck out. He then moved to Illinois where he married, started a family, and served in an Illinois regiment of the Union Army during the Civil War.

Bolton was an excellent soldier, earning the rank of sergeant during his brief hitch, and eventually being commissioned as an officer. He distinguished himself on the battlefield on more than one occasion, but Bolton became known for something quite peculiar during his time in the military—he hated horses!

It may seem like a strange thing for an Old West outlaw to hate horses, but as we'll see, it didn't slow down Black Bart. After he was discharged from the Army, Bolton returned to his family in Illinois for several years, but his traveling bone brought him out west once again to look for gold.

He intended to return to his family. However, in August 1871, he wrote his wife a letter in which he claimed to have had problems with some Wells Fargo security agents. He promised to get revenge on them.

Bolton put on a hood and took to robbing Wells Fargo stagecoaches in California and Oregon. Several things separated him from most other outlaws of the period: he worked alone, he never rode a horse, and he was always quite gentlemanly. Bart made sure to never swear at his victims and he never fired his pistols. On two occasions he even left poems. One of them read:

"I've labored long and hard for bread/ For honor and for riches/ But on my corns too long you've tred/ You fine haired Sons of Bitches." It was signed "Black Bart."

Black Bart was finally captured in 1884 and served four years in the famous San Quentin Prison. When Black Bart was released in 1888, the mystery of his life only deepened. He was last seen in California's Central Valley, but after that, he was never heard from again.

Some said he went to New York City where he lived anonymously until 1917 (I'm not sure how anonymous it could've been if people knew he was there). Other people believed he tried to strike it rich one last time panning for gold and died somewhere in the mountains. A Wells Fargo agent swore that he retired to Japan for some reason. Whatever happened to Black Bart, his sudden disappearance only added to his already fascinating legend.

So, there you have it. There were two Black Barts. Only one went by the moniker during his lifetime, however.

Conclusion

I hope you enjoyed reading *Interesting Stories for Curious People: A Fascinating Collection of Stories Relating to History, Pop Culture, Science, and Just About Anything Else You Can Think Of*, Part Two. You were introduced to some pretty engaging and informative material, so you're ready to go out and try your new trivia knowledge on your family, friends, and coworkers.

You no doubt have some favorite stories or groups of stories from the book. Perhaps you were most fascinated by learning about how the legends of frontier outlaws kept circulating, and even increased, long after their deaths. Those men certainly lived interesting lives and their deaths were just as captivating and definitely more mysterious.

Maybe you were more intrigued by the weird science facts in this book. Some of those science stories may seem too strange to be true, but now you know that they are all 100% science fact and not science fiction.

With that said, many people are drawn to stories of the supernatural, parapsychology, and cryptozoology. There are so many odd occurrences and phenomena in our world that defy any logical explanation. You've read about a few of those in this book and now you can impress others with that information.

Of course, this wouldn't be a true trivia book if it didn't have information about sports and pop culture. And just to make sure things were always interesting, we threw in plenty of stories about serial killers, capers, and criminals for all you true crime fans.

There is no doubt that there is something for everyone in this book, but since you've read it, you already know that. So, take the knowledge you gained from this book, have fun with it, and bring it out into the world. But be careful, always be aware of your surroundings, and always consider what you're doing because we wouldn't want you to be the next entry of *Interesting Stories for Curious People*!

DON'T FORGET YOUR FREE BOOKS

MORE BOOKS BY BILL O'NEILL

I hope you enjoyed this book and learned
something new. Please feel free to check out
some of my previous books on Amazon.

Printed in Great Britain
by Amazon